MONSTER GARAGE™

HOW TO
WELD
DAMN NEAR ANYTHING

DISCOVERY CHANNEL™

Entertain your brain™

MOTORBOOKS
INTERNATIONAL

This edition first published in 2004 by Motorbooks International, an imprint of MBI Publishing Company, Galtier Plaza, Suite 200, 380 Jackson Street, St. Paul, MN 55101-3885 USA

Motorbooks International titles are also available at discounts in bulk quantity for industrial or sales-promotional use. For details write to Special Sales Manager at Motorbooks International Wholesalers & Distributors, Galtier Plaza, Suite 200, 380 Jackson Street, St. Paul, MN 55101-3885 USA.

ISBN 0-7603-1808-5

On the frontispiece: Jesse James on the set of Monster Garage. *Discovery Channel*

On the title page: The Grim Reaper was a Monster project gone awry. The hearse was going to be converted into a car-crushing beast. It didn't work. Talk on the set was that the car was haunted. Discovery Channel *Discovery Channel*

On the back cover: Top: Lisa Legohn, a master welder who appeared on the Firetruck episode, lights her weapon of choice. Discovery Channel Bottom: This 1987 Winnebago was transformed into a skate park in the Road Ramp episode. *Discovery Channel*

Discovery Communications development team:
Clark Bunting II, General Manager,
    Discovery Channel
Sharon M. Bennett, Senior Vice President,
    Strategic Partnerships & Licensing
Thom Beers, Executive Producer,
    Original Productions
Sean Gallagher, Director of Programming Development,
    Discovery Channel
David McKillop, Executive Producer,
    Discovery Channel
Deidre Scott, Vice President,
    Licensing
Carol Le Blanc, Vice President of Marketing
    and Retail Development
Jeannine Gaubert, Designer, Licensing
Erica Jacobs Green, Publishing Manager

Acquisitions Editor: Lee Klancher
Associate Editor: Leah Noel
Art directed by Rochelle L. Schultz
Designed by Brenda C. Canales

CONTENTS

PREFACE

You are likely reading *How to Weld Damn Near Anything* because you want to create first-class metal fabrication with a welder. Certified-quality performance welding can be used to improve any welding project. Projects like motocross racing bicycles with aluminum or titanium frames, custom motorcycles, racing go karts, and stainless-steel railings for ocean-going yachts will all benefit from the very best welding.

So, what is the difference between regular welding and performance welding? Here is a good example of regular welding: You might be able to build an attractive utility trailer to tow snowmobiles, but the welds on your trailer are about 50 percent cold and 50 percent penetrated. No problem. The trailer will stay together.

Welding takes on a whole different level of importance when the demands on the bond increase. If you are driving a race car at 200 miles per hour into turn one at Phoenix International Raceway, for example, your welds need to be rock solid. Or if you are flying an experimental airplane at a 10,500-foot altitude over the forests of the Upper Peninsula of Michigan, you want the engine mount to have 100 percent reliable welds. In race cars and airplanes, you can't tolerate anything less than perfect welds. In boat trailers and farm and garden equipment, you can get by with a few defects in your welds, but in performance welding for metal assemblies that really count, you must be very, very good at what you do.

This book will tell you, step-by-step, how to make perfect welds every time. There will be no more 50 percent welds unless you want 50 percent welds. So read on, and become a performance welder.

The following people need to be thanked for their contributions to this book: Edward G. Morgan, district manager, Lincoln Electric Company; Hal Olcott, district manager, Victor Equipment Company; Karl Grimm, branch manager, Air Liquide Corporation; Rick Wachner, branch manager, So-Cal Airgas Corporation; Kirk Merica, district manager, Miller Electric Company; and Laurie Longanecker, word processor, B-R Word Processing.

On the Discovery Channel series *Monster Garage*, a team of talented fabricators, designers, and specialists come together to transform ordinary vehicles into fantastic machines. A key part of this transformation is shaping and working with metal, and welding is perhaps the most crucial skill of a good fabricator.

Welding bonds metal to metal, and a good welder can fix damn near anything that is metal with a few scrap pieces and some ingenuity. In this book, you will learn not only the basics of how to bond metal to metal with an electric arc, but you will also learn the newest techniques used to bond high-strength, lightweight metals used in race cars and aircraft.

How to Weld Damn Near Anything covers the basic techniques of welding, from "stick" welding through to more sophisticated methods such as MIG and TIG welding. This book will not only give the reader a solid grounding in the basics of welding, but it will also introduce methods that can be used in high-end custom projects to bond lighter, stronger metals.

OBSOLETE INFORMATION

In several other books that supposedly gave instruction in aircraft-quality welding, most of the chapters and reprinted articles were copyrighted or published in the 1930s and occasionally in the late 1950s. Airplanes and race cars have changed dramatically since 1935. Major technological discoveries have created greatly improved processes in almost all areas of transportation and sports. Improvements in metallurgy have allowed major leaps in every aspect of material strength and fatigue resistance since the 1930s and 1950s. *How to Weld Damn Near Anything* takes into consideration these recent technological developments and enables you to use the most recent and up-to-date methods and materials in your welding projects.

And if you are building a new-structure airplane or race car, you need to take full advantage of the most current and up-to-date welding procedures.

This book will teach you the very latest procedures in TIG (tungsten inert gas) welding, MIG (metal inert gas) welding, and OFW (oxy-fuel) welding, and it will review recent major advances in filler metals (welding rod and wire).

RACE CAR FACTORIES

Most, but not all, Indy race car teams use the very best welding rod and the very latest welding equipment. In the "Indy Car Rule Book," certain types of welding repairs are restricted, as are certain types of chassis and suspension member construction. For instance, in the early 1970s, many racing accidents were caused by cracked suspension castings. As a result, castings were banned from race-car suspension members. Only forged or welded suspension members were allowed. The race-car industry was actually ahead of the aircraft industry in metallurgy and welding technology, and still is, in many respects.

OLD RUMORS

For many years, welding advice has been passed by word-of-mouth from older welders to younger welders. Much of this handed-down information has been misleading or flat-out wrong.

Techniques such as relieving post-welding stress with an oxyacetylene torch, welding with scrap wire, and other procedures with no scientific basis were erroneously passed on to newer welders. Using metallurgical facts, this book debunks these ineffective techniques.

The end result is that you will be able to accomplish high-quality welding on aerospace materials, and your welds won't break! Now, let's explore the three high-quality welding processes.

For more information on Monster Garage, go to Discovery.com.

COMPARING WELDING PROCESSES:

TIG, MIG AND OXYACETYLENE

The amateur welder has a number of welding options available. The key to deciding what kind of welder is right for your own personal Monster Garage is determining your welding needs.

The three kinds of welding dealt with in this chapter are TIG welding, MIG welding, and gas welding. Oxyacetylene gas welding is the oldest of these processes, and was used to weld together mild steel tubing in 1930s-era aircraft.

Heliarc welding came next, generally in the mid- to late 1950s. But Heliarc welding equipment was relatively expensive and very bulky at first.

Wire-feed welding, now called MIG welding, first became popular for heavy-duty welding in the auto industry, when manufacturers used this process to mass-produce car and truck frames.

The descriptions below will help you decide which welding process best suits your finances and your intended projects.

TIG WELDING

In TIG welding, a very-high-temperature, but very confined, arc heats the base metal to the melting point for the purpose of fusion welding.

TIG welding uses less heat to join metal than either MIG or gas welding. TIG welding is by far the most controllable of all manual (not automatic) welding processes. It is so accurate that you could weld a thin piece of 0.010-inch steel sheet to a thick piece of 6.000-inch steel billet and not burn through the thin sheet, yet get good penetration into the thick billet.

In fact, TIG welding allows for fusion welding without the addition of filler rod, making it possible to produce welds without extra weld seam buildup. And with a foot-pedal amp control or a thumb amp control on the TIG torch, you can actually strike an arc, start a tiny weld puddle, and, without moving the puddle or adding welding rod, maintain the same weld molten puddle for minutes or even hours at a time. That is how controllable TIG welding is.

The advantage to such precise puddle control is to provide adequate time to properly add filler rod material to the puddle. You can strike an arc, form a puddle, then you can carefully and accurately add just the right amount of filler rod at exactly the right place in the molten weld puddle.

MIG WELDING

Commonly called wire-feed welding because a thin wire is fed into the weld puddle by an electric motor-drive system, this emerging process is quickly gaining in popularity because it is easy to operate and relatively fast. A TIG welder can weld about 6 inches of 0.050-inch steel sheet in one minute, whereas a MIG welder can weld up to 24 inches of the same material in one minute.

There are pros and cons to MIG welding the more exotic thin-wall 4130 steel tubes and thin sheets of 4130 steel used in aircraft construction. Here are some of the considerations:

PROS OF MIG WELDING

It is easy to turn the power switch on, turn the gas on, and merely point the gun and pull the trigger to wire-feed weld race car frames and aircraft fuselage structures. It is possible to weld a lot more inches of weld bead per hour with MIG welding than with any other welding process. The reason is that the welding filler metal is continuously fed from a spool of wire into the weld for as long as the welder holds the welding gun trigger.

A MIG weld bead is usually a very sound weld, almost as sound as a perfectly done TIG weld. Once the amps, volts, and wire-feed speed are properly adjusted, MIG welding is a very high-quality welding process.

CONS OF MIG WELDING

Several problems associated with MIG welding include the normal tendency of an electrode-fed arc weld to start off cold. This means that each start of the arc is not fully penetrated for the first fractions of an inch of weld bead. Once the MIG weld bead is established, the heat and penetration is normal, but it always starts off cold.

Another disadvantage to MIG welding is that the process is highly intolerant of any gaps in the fit-up of the parts. MIG wire is usually 0.025 inch to 0.030 inch in diameter, and if there is a gap larger than the diameter of the electrode, the wire can slip into the crack and fail to make a weld bead. Another disadvantage of welding small-diameter thin-wall tubing with MIG is that once you accidentally burn a hole in the tubing, it is very hard to fill the hole without stopping to make a patch for it. There may also be times you will have to use gas welding to patch holes made by MIG welding.

The primary difficulty with MIG welding is that once you squeeze the trigger on the MIG gun, you are committed to move along with making a weld bead, ready or not. If you make a bad start, sometimes you have to stop, grind or cut out the weld bead, and then start over again.

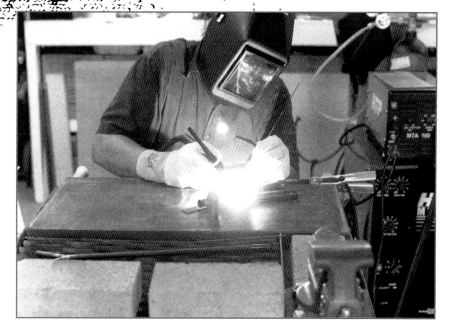

TIG welding is the easiest, cleanest, and most precise of all manual-welding methods. In this photo, a towbar bracket is being TIG tack welded using a modular MIG-TIG welder. *Richard Finch*

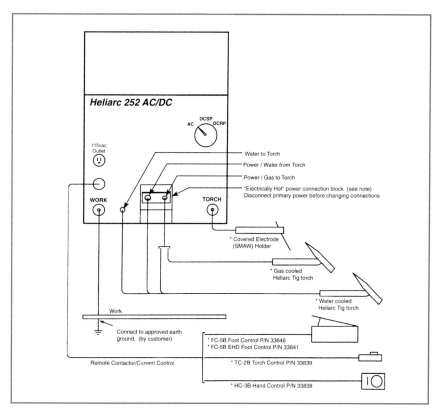

In this illustration, you can see the schematic of a TIG welding setup. *ESAB Welding & Cutting Products*

GAS WELDING

The oldest aircraft welding process is still good and dependable. Oxyacetylene welding is very much the same as it was in 1920. The two gases, oxygen and the fuel gas acetylene, are still the same as they have been for 100 years or more. Gas welding torches have slowly evolved over the years, but a torch made 50 years ago would still be a dependable welding torch. And gas welding rigs are still the least expensive of all welding setups. Chapter 2 explains the best ones to have.

The neutral flame combines an equal pressure of oxygen and acetylene to produce a flame temperature at the inner core of about 5,000°F, a temperature that is also used in TIG welding. The difference is that the oxyacetylene flame produces fewer BTUs (British thermal units, a measurement of heat units) and much more lower-temperature heat at its outer flame.

What this means is that in the process of welding a butt joint of thin-wall tubing, the heat-affected area of the tube will be several times larger with gas welding than with TIG or MIG welding. But this is

Typical MIG or wire-feed welding setups require these basic elements for operation.
Lincoln Electric Company

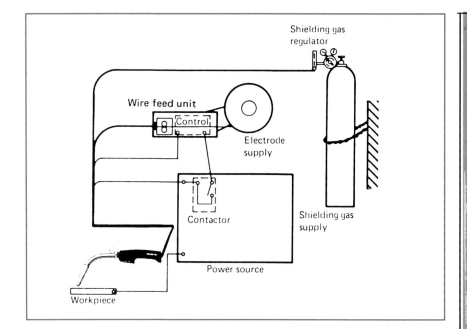

Gas-welding setups have not changed much since the early years. This drawing shows a typical commercial oxyacetylene welding rig used in the 1930s. *Richard Finch Collection*

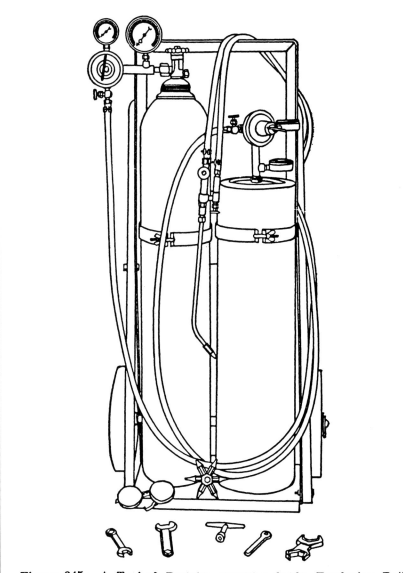

Figure 245.—A Typical Portable Welding Outfit, Employing Both Welding Gases (Oxygen and Acetylene) in Safety Storage Cylinders, Mounted on a Two-Wheeled Truck. This Outfit Weighs Less Than 300 Lbs., and May Be Handled Easily by One Man.

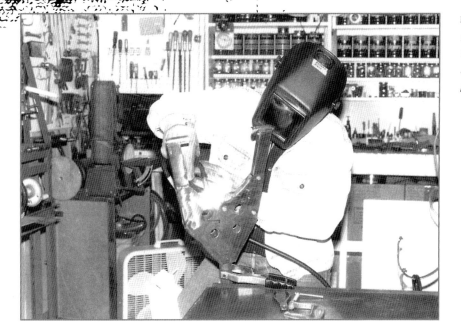

seldom a problem. The gas welding flame does heat the assembly more, but in steel and aluminum in thicknesses of less than 0.100 inch, the gas welding torch is very adequate.

There are a few difficulties with gas welding. When you are attempting to weld inside corners, the flame is blown back toward you, and that makes the heat on your hands uncomfortable. Another difficulty is in welding next to an edge of tubing or plate. The heat of the torch is considerably broader than with TIG or MIG welding, and this causes sharp edges to melt away. The solution is to add extra length to the metal joint to be welded and then trim it to the correct size after completing the weld.

RACE CAR WELDING

TIG welding is nearly the exclusive choice in the construction of Formula One, Indy cars, Indy Lights, and the smaller formula cars such as Formula Ford and Super Vee classes.

The reason for this is the relatively small number of cars built in each of these classes. TIG welding is the most accurate of all welding processes, and with fewer cars to build, it doesn't matter that it takes a little longer to fabricate suspension and systems parts.

In this chapter, look at the photo of the front suspension of Michael Andretti's backup Indy race car. It is made from 4130 steel tubing that has threaded inserts TIG welded in each end. MIG welding would

From left to right, these aircraft-grade 4130 tube assemblies were welded by (1) TIG, (2) MIG, and (3) gas. TIG is more accurate and is cleaner. MIG is fast and less accurate. Gas is slow and somewhat less accurate, but reasonably priced. *Richard Finch*

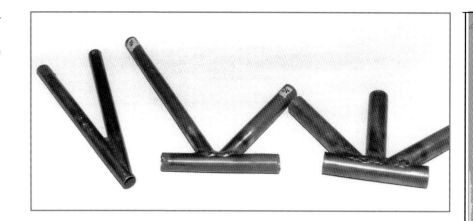

Race car driver Michael Andretti's backup Indy race car makes use of TIG welding in the very delicate but strong front suspension. Most of the welding on his car is by the TIG process. *Richard Finch*

not be adequate for those spindly looking suspension tubes because MIG welding cannot be controlled accurately enough to make 100 percent sound welds.

In the photo of the Jim Russell Formula Ford race car in this chapter, note the smooth, accurate TIG welds in the frame and suspension. Again, MIG welding would have been less adequate here because of the need for 100 percent accurate welds. And it's easy to see in the photo of the Buick V-6 Indy Lights radiator installation that gas or MIG welding would not have been easy or sound, if possible at all.

AIRCRAFT MIG WELDING

Many aircraft fuselages have been MIG welded in the past 25 or 30 years. The process obviously works, and there have been few, if any, problems with MIG-welded airplanes or components.

Although it may seem that the need to start welding cold and to weld a steady, straight bead would be a problem in small-diameter thin-wall round tubing, there are techniques (as explained in chapter seven) to do this. Quantity production often requires construction methods that are faster than possible with MIG welding.

RACE CAR MIG WELDING

Certain racing classes depend on a few chassis constructors to build a relatively large number of race car rolling chassises. The need to provide dozens of tube-frame race car chassis dictates that the very

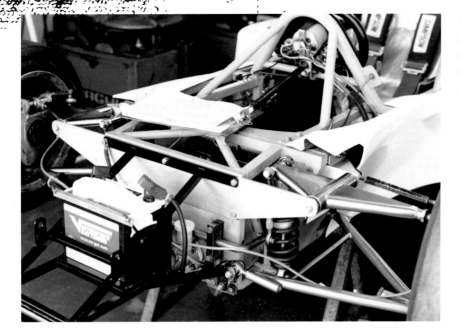

Most of the frame and lightweight fabricated front suspension on this Jim Russell Driving School Formula Ford car is TIG welded for strength and neatness. *Richard Finch*

In the left of this photo you can see the TIG-welded aluminum radiator filler tank on this Buick V-6 Indy Lights race car. The TIG-welded exhaust system is complicated, but actually easy to fabricate by proper fitting and TIG welding. *Richard Finch*

fastest fabrication methods be used. MIG welding is the answer.

AIRCRAFT GAS WELDING

For low-production airplane fuselage construction, a good-quality oxyacetylene welding rig is very adequate. The large number of certified airplanes still flying 50 to 75 years after being welded with gas is a strong statement in favor of gas welding as a good, safe welding process.

Many airplane designs are available today with gas-welded rudder pedal assemblies, engine mounts, and complete fuselage assemblies. When properly performed, gas welding is perfectly adequate, and it is easy to do properly. Read more in chapters 9 and 10 about gas welding.

On this Aerostar S/N266, the engine mounts, all turbocharger brackets, the stainless-steel exhaust waste gates, the aluminum air boxes, and the gas heater exhaust were all TIG welded. The six seat frames were MIG welded. Silver solder was used to make strong electrical connections at the rear-mounted dual 12-volt batteries. *Richard Finch*

From the mid-1970s on, Bellanca Viking airplanes featured MIG-welded fuselages, tail structures, and landing-gear assemblies. Prior to about 1975, they were welded by TIG and gas processes. *Richard Finch*

Bellanca Citabria aerobatic airplanes feature MIG-welded 4130 steel-tube fuselage and tail structures. A completed Citabria is in the background. *Richard Finch*

This close-up picture of an aircraft door frame shows the welding detail of the MIG-welded tubular structure, the door-hinge plates, and the finger doublers that make this a very strong airplane fuselage. *Richard Finch*

This fiberglass-fuselage Glastar experimental airplane employs riveted aluminum wings and tail and a MIG- and TIG-welded 4130 steel-tube structural frame under the fuselage's fiberglass skin. *Richard Finch*

This VW Scirocco class-SSB race car complied with SCCA racing rules with the addition of a TIG-welded roll cage, TIG-welded window net brackets, and TIG-welded five-point seat-belt restraint brackets. *Richard Finch*

Most of the frame welding on this race car is by the MIG process. *Richard Finch*

Stick (arc) welding was used to attach the brake drum backing plate adapter ring to the axle on this 1938 airplane wheel assembly. Arc welding has been obsolete for aircraft assembly since MIG and TIG processes were invented in 1955 and 1945, respectively. *Richard Finch*

This World War II observation airplane axle assembly was fabricated by gas welding. This process is still viable and structurally adequate for similar aircraft. *Richard Finch*

CHAPTER
2

SHOPPING
FOR
welding
EQUIPMENT

Your first welder will be a very special purchase. This is a tool that will serve you well on rebuilding and repair projects. In fact, owning a welder is a bit of a rite of passage. The line, "Yes, I own a welder," elicits instant status when casually dropped at BBQs, and other gatherings where people congregate around cooking meat or the cooler.

Before you start shopping for welding equipment, determine your budget so you'll know what you can afford. In this chapter, you'll learn about your choices and get suggestions about where to look for equipment.

You should know up front that there are cheap welders sold by stores that can't even tell you how to use the machines. You can buy arc welders for less than $100 and MIG welders for less than $200. These machines will make you think that welding is an art you can't master. Leave them at the store where you found them. If you did accidentally buy one, it is extremely unlikely that you could ever find repair parts, and it is highly unlikely that you could even get it to work the way it is advertised.

MAIL-ORDER WELDERS

Make sure you can return any piece of welding equipment if it will not perform as advertised. But don't wait too long to request a return. Companies frown on people who buy equipment for a project, use it, then ask for a refund.

USED WELDERS

One local college recently shut down its entire machine shop program and sold all the machinery at 10 percent of acquisition cost. A very large aviation corporation in this same area recently went out of business, and they auctioned everything, including several high-quality TIG welders. They sold for 10 to 20 percent of original acquisition cost. Good-quality name-brand welding equipment should last for 50 years or more if properly maintained. Consider buying used equipment if your budget is limited.

NEW TECHNOLOGY

We are all familiar with recent technological innovations in consumer electronics, including cellular telephones, personal computers, and home entertainment systems. Similar technological innovations have affected the welding industry. More about this later, but you need to know where to go to find out about the very latest in welding technology.

TENT SALES

Tent sales are great places to see new technology and to get bargains on great name-brand welding equipment. Tent sales are usually held in parking lots of established welding-supply businesses.

SQUARE-WAVE TECHNOLOGY

Welding equipment technology has advanced significantly, and square-wave technology is now available to provide a very smooth output-welding arc in AC aluminum- and magnesium-welding modes. Square-wave technology also smoothes out the DC welding output when welding steel, stainless steel, and titanium. Do not buy a new TIG or MIG welding machine until you have compared square-wave technology with earlier AC/DC equipment. My guess is that you'll choose one of the square-wave welders, which are now manufactured by all name-brand welder companies.

NAME BRANDS

Over the 10 years countless welding companies have been sold and merged with other companies, often forming companies with new names. The same phenomenon is still happening today. Recently, two long-time, well-known welding equipment manufacturers, Miller Electric Manufacturing Company and Hobart Brothers Company, merged under the management of Illinois Tool Works. Also under the same management are PowCon, Oxo, Tri Mark, Corex, and McKay, other long-time companies in the welding business. So it's wise for anyone who wants to stay current in the welding field to visit American Welding Society meetings, visit your local welding trade schools, and attend at least two or three welding trade shows every year.

PORTABLE RIGS

Trailer- or truck-mounted portable welding rigs are rapidly becoming a thing of the past. New inverter technology makes it possible to carry a pipe-welding-capacity power supply not much larger than your arc-welding helmet in the trunk of your car. Not many inverter welders will weld aluminum or magnesium, but that has started to change.

MODULAR ADD-ONS

For about half the price of the lowest-cost TIG welder, you can purchase a modular TIG add-on that features capacitor start or, in some products, high-frequency

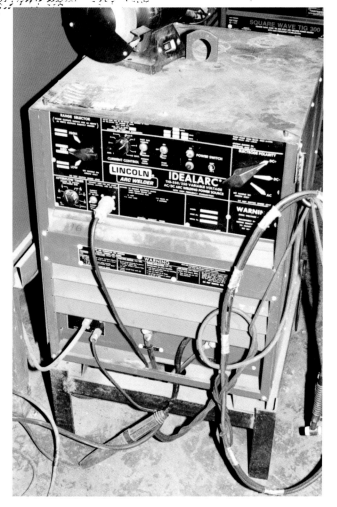

You can buy a very good, dependable TIG stick welder like this one at company closings and school closeout sales. This Lincoln Idealarc is a very good TIG welder, but it lacks the newer square-wave features. The usual price is $200 to $400 used. *Richard Finch*

Tent sales like this one at a welding supply outlet are good places to find sale prices and try out the latest equipment. *Richard Finch*

(the best) start. This means that if you have a good old stick welder or a good old wire-feed welder, you can use its transformer to power a TIG torch, even with a foot-pedal control and argon-gas timing.

ELECTRONIC WELDING HELMETS

For many years, welders who did stick, TIG, and MIG welding were forced to aim the torch, stick, or gun at the weld with their helmets up, then shake their head to lower their helmet, and hope their aim at the weld joint had not moved. This problem was the biggest obstacle to learning to weld quickly. Even old-timers never really mastered the flip-the-helmet-down trick. You always had to stop welding, raise the helmet, and look to see if you had made a good weld.

Very recently, some savvy engineer designed an electronic welding lens that is a shade 3 (sunglasses shade) when no welding arc is present. The lens shade changes to a 10, 11, or 12 as soon as an arc is struck, but the change is not instantaneous. You do see the arc, but only for about 1/500 to 1/125,000 of a second. What this means is that at the end of a long day of arc welding, your eyes will itch about as much as if you had spent the day at the beach without sunglasses. These helmets run from $100 to $275 or more. They really do contribute to much more accurate arc starts in stick, TIG, and MIG welding, as well as plasma arc cutting.

TIG TORCHES

Just like ballpoint pens, TIG torches come in many sizes and qualities. A small water-cooled torch is best for most aircraft welding, and a torch that can be adapted to gas-lens operation is the best kind. Several good brands of TIG torches are on the market, and the best way to shop for a torch is to ask to see a selection of collets, chucks, and cups for the particular torch you are looking at. If you can buy a full range of collets from 0.020 inch up to 5/32 inch, then you can expect good service from that torch. If parts are not available, don't even think about buying it.

THUMB CONTROLS

You will not always be able to TIG weld at tabletop level. Some welds must be reached by standing on a ladder or by crouching 6 inches off the floor. For many years, the solution to these hard-to-reach TIG welds was to lay a brick on the foot pedal and hope for the right amount of heat from the torch or to go find a

One of the newer square-wave AC/DC TIG and SAW (stick) welding machines is this 175-pound, 175-amp square-wave welder that sells for $1,300, complete with all accessories except a cart and an argon bottle. *Richard Finch*

The next step up in a TIG welder is this electronic-control-panel square-wave 255-amp TIG welding machine. As shown here with a closed-loop radiator and two argon bottles, expect to spend about $3,500 for the complete outfit. *Richard Finch*

helper to push the pedal for you. Welds made this way were never as good as they could have been.

The solution to this TIG welding problem is to buy a thumb- or forefinger-operated TIG amp control switch that you attach to your TIG torch with Velcro. You won't use the thumb- or finger-control TIG switch much, but when you need it, you'll be happy you have it.

CONSUMABLES

Products consumed in the course of welding are called consumables. They include welding and brazing rod, wire on spools, flux for brazing, solder and pastes for soldering, and even MIG gun parts, plasma-cutter parts, TIG cups, and tungsten. Appendix A, "Welding Supplies: Rods, Wires, Fluxes," covers consumables.

EXTRA FLOWMETER

For less than $90, you can buy a spare flowmeter to make back-gas purges of stainless-steel and titanium welds. The price of the extra flowmeter is so low that just one critical weld project will pay for it. This is not a starting-kit item, because you might weld for many hours before you ever need to back-gas purge something, but when a stainless-steel or titanium weld project comes up, by all means invest in a spare flowmeter.

GAS WELDERS

Don't buy the cheapest discount-store or mail-order torch you can find. Stick with brand names like Thermadyne (formerly Victor), Lincoln (formerly Harris), and Smiths. For a second torch, you might want to

Tim Marr, an expert welder, proudly shows a top-of-the-line Lincoln square-wave 355-amp TIG and stick welder that has numerous extra features. This machine sells for $3,600 without cart, cooler, and argon cylinders, making the cost for a complete unit about $4,500. *Richard Finch*

The dream of many home shop welders—and a great portable weld rig as well is this 190-amp TIG welder that runs off 110-volt house current or 220-volt shop current. It's a DC-only welder that sells for about $1,500, but it only weighs 19 pounds! *Richard Finch*

The real Heliarc welders, made by ESAB Welding & Cutting Products of Florence, South Carolina. These 255-amp and 352-amp TIG and stick welders also feature square-wave technology. *ESAB Welding & Cutting Products*

investigate the pistol-grip Dillon/Henrob model. Go to welding sales. One loss leader at tent sales is the portable hand-carried gas welding and cutting rig. Make sure you can buy extra tips and extra rosebud tips for any torch you buy. No spare parts should mean no sale!

SHOP TOOLS

Every weld shop must have one or more air-operated cut-off tools and a small angle sander. Tubing benders are a necessity, and several new models are available. Many new benders feature hand-operated hydraulic jacks to make smooth, wrinkle-free bends in thin-wall tubing. Most of these tubing benders can be purchased by mail. Suppliers' addresses and phone numbers can be found in race car and aircraft builders' magazines.

PLASMA CUTTERS

Any welding shop that uses a TIG or MIG welder for even two hours a day would benefit from a plasma cutter. The only efficient way to cut stainless steel of any thickness from 0.020 inch up to 3/8 inch is with an air-operated plasma cutter.

Daytona MIG Company specializes in mail-order sales of this Pocket Pulse DC-only TIG welder and the 110-volt Pocket Plasma Cutter, which are useful for small shops or as backup machines in larger fabrication shops. *Richard Finch*

These machines cut pencil-thin kerfs in any metal, and they leave very little dross or slag on the backside of the cut. Any shop that fabricates mild-steel or stainless-steel exhaust systems absolutely must have a plasma cutter, especially for cutting 3/16-inch and 1/4-inch flanges for the pipes.

Plasma cutters are available in 110-, 220-, and 440-volt versions. Mail-order welding supply companies all feature 110-volt plasma cutters, but some of the less-expensive cutters must be push-started, which is not very useful. Remember the motto, "Try it before you buy it," or make sure you get a satisfaction guarantee.

This 220-volt Pocket Pulse TIG machine is made in Italy and sold by Daytona MIG Company through ads in car magazines. *Richard Finch*

RETAIL WELDING STORES

Much like car dealerships, service after the sale is more important than the initial purchase. Check out at least three or four local dealers before you decide where to do business. Retail welding stores vary widely in service even before the sale. Don't fence yourself in to dealing with a bad dealer.

Electronic welding helmets let the welder see the TIG, MIG or stick at a sunglasses number 3 tint before striking the arc. They change to number 10, 11 or 12 lens tint within 1/100,000 of a second after the arc is started. They cost between $125 and $350. *Richard Finch*

The backside of the Jackson electronic welding helmet shows the five buttons that adjust the helmet's operating shades. *Richard Finch*

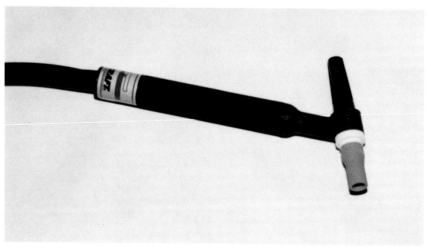

A TIG torch is this Weldcraft WP-10 torch with a short back cap. This water-cooled torch will weld up to 1/4-inch-thick aluminum and steel. *Richard Finch*

The TIG torch thumb control starts and stops this large water-cooled torch without the need for a foot control. You cannot operate a TIG foot control when you are on your knees trying to weld something one foot off the floor. *Richard Finch*

Every TIG welder needs to ask Santa Claus to bring him one of these TIG Cradles. It conveniently holds *all* the TIG parts a welder needs. *Richard Finch*

An often-forgotten accessory for a TIG welder is a second argon flowmeter for back-gas purging stainless-steel and titanium welds. *Richard Finch*

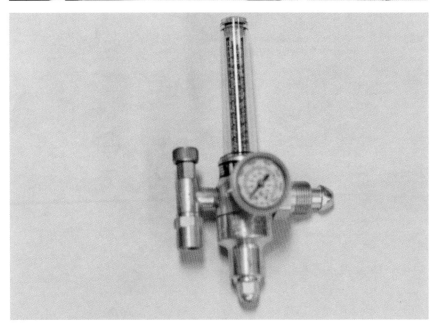

This heavy-duty TIG- or MIG-torch water pump pays for itself by recirculating cooling water rather than wasting the water down the drain. *Richard Finch*

This closed-circuit coolant radiator is built for water-cooled TIG and MIG torches. *Richard Finch*

This 150-pound Econotig welder does AC/DC TIG welds as well as stick welds. *Richard Finch*

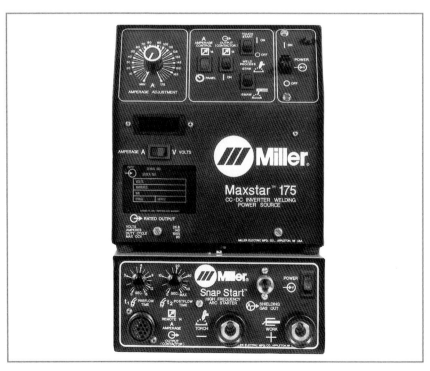

Becoming more popular are these modular units that allow fabrication shops to tailor their welding equipment to their needs. *Miller Electric Company*

For repeatable high-quality TIG, MIG, and stick welding, some manufacturers provide a full control panel on their arc-welding power source. *Miller Electric Company*

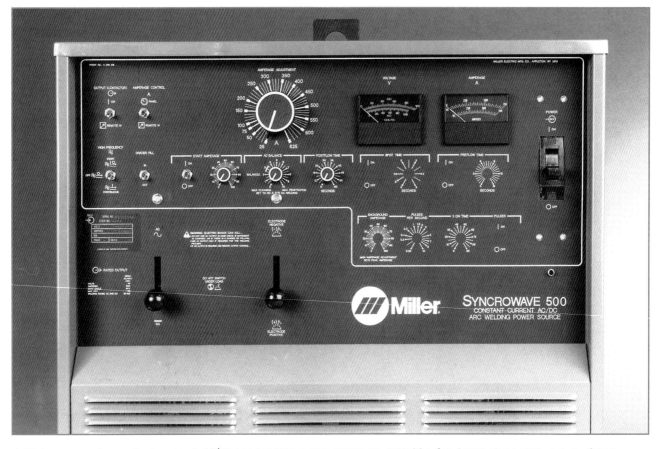

A higher-powered, constant-current AC/DC arc-welding power source is suitable for large shops with a lot of big welding jobs. *Miller Electric Company*

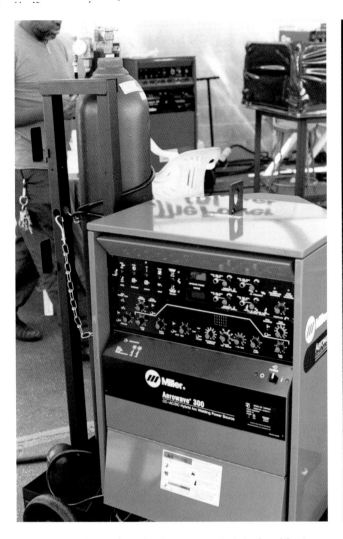

A high-tech TIG welder that is purported to be able to
weld aluminum engine blocks back together with ease.
Cost: $6,000. *Richard Finch*

Every welding shop, regardless of size or welding
capability, should have one of these portable gas
welding/cutting/heating rigs. The total cost of this outfit
with two gas bottles and the cart is $395. *Richard Finch*

Portable plasma cutters are a time- and money-saving investment if your shop spends two hours a day in metal fabrication.
ESAB Welding & Cutting Products

This new air-operated die grinder and cut-off wheel was purchased for $15. Every shop should have one or more of these. *Richard Finch*

Defective welds are easily cut out with an air-operated die grinder, as the welder is doing here on a Lycoming engine mount. *Wag-Aero Group*

Buy several of these magnetic angle jigs. Once you use one, you'll be addicted. *Richard Finch*

FITTING and CLEANING

A properly fitted and cleaned weld assembly makes the welding process much easier and more sound than a poorly fitted, dirty assembly. Fitting is the most time-consuming part of welding any assembly, but fitting is also the major contributor to good high-quality welds.

A nuclear power plant welding inspector noticed that the pipe fitters did about 80 percent of the work, and the higher-paid welders did only 20 percent of the work in fabricating the piping in the nuclear power plant. You will find the same time ratio in fitting and welding aircraft or race car assemblies.

FILE TO FIT

Numerous books on pipe and tube welding offer many solutions to fishmouthing tubing. Some welders actually dress several widths of abrasive grinding wheels to a half-circle, and grind the fishmouth into each tube end! Others try to band-saw the fishmouth into the tube, then finish the notch with a half-round file. Still others mount a milling cutter in a lathe and push the tube into the cutter, which can be rather dangerous.

HOLE SAW

Then some clever fabricator designed a hole-saw mandrel and an adjustable tubing clamp assembly and revolutionized the fitting of tubing for welding. In the photos in this chapter, you can see how easy it is to cut tubing to the exact angle and the exact fishmouth size. The entire process to set up, for example, a 52-degree angle cut in a piece of 1.50-inch x 0.95-inch wall thickness tube is about one minute. The actual cut takes even less time.

After the hole-saw fishmouth cut is made, there will be burrs around the saw cut that must be removed with a file or a sanding belt. The area to be welded must then be sanded clean of mill scale and cleaned with acetone before the weld is made.

FITTING THE PARTS BEFORE WELDING

The fit-up of tubing or parts to be welded is the most essential part of weld preparation. Do a good fit-up and your weld will be much easier to do, and it will be stronger and prettier!

Fit every part to have a gap that's less than the thickness of the welding rod being used. In most cases, the gap between aircraft parts to be welded should be less than 0.020 inch. If the welding rod can be inserted between the parts, the fit-up is less than ideal and is too loose for a good, strong weld.

Wide gaps can be filled, but bridging open air between the parts causes hot spots in the weld, and the air gap on the backside of the weld allows atmospheric contaminants such as hydrogen and oxygen to weaken and crack the weld. These wide gaps in the weld will cause fatigue cracking in the weld at a later time. Hidden hot cracking often occurs in poorly fitted joints.

Weld joints will last a lifetime if properly designed and fitted before welding. Take an extra 5 or 10 minutes and fit the joints properly.

Tubing joints can be fitted perfectly if you use one of the hole-saw tubing notchers that are on the market. They sell for $149 to $279, and can make fitting tubes much easier than filing and grinding each fishmouth by hand.

CAUTION

When using a bi-metal hole saw to fishmouth steel tubing less than 1 inch in diameter and with less than 0.049-inch wall thickness, be aware of the fact that the coarse hole-saw blade teeth can shatter if special care is not taken to cut very slowly. You must engage the saw into the tubing very slowly to avoid shattering all the teeth off the hole-saw blade.

Quite likely, some enterprising manufacturer will see the opportunity to make a special bi-metal hole saw for cutting thin-wall tubing. Ideally, a 1/2-inch diameter hole saw should have 15 teeth per inch rather than the six or eight teeth per inch that is currently available. Meanwhile, cut small, thin tubes slowly.

CLEAN THE PARTS THOROUGHLY BEFORE WELDING

All new metal will have oil and scale on 4130 steel, stainless steel, and aluminum will not be ready to weld as it comes to you from the supplier. Stainless steel will have oil or even protective paper and sticky glue on it. Aluminum will have oil or paper or aluminum oxide on it, and 4130 chrome-moly steel will have pickling oil and mill scale on it when it comes to you. This "dirt" will contaminate the weld if it is not removed prior to welding.

All old, used, repairable metal will have paint, oil, rust, corrosion, and oxidation on it. This dirt absolutely

must be cleaned off before welding. Dirt contaminates and weakens welds.

RECOMMENDED CLEANING METHODS PRIOR TO WELDING

Chrome-moly steel (4130) must be sanded to a bright, new-appearing metal under the gray mill scale on the surface of the tubing, 4130 steel sheet, or plate. The mill scale must be cleaned off 1 inch back from the edge to be welded. Tubing can be hand sanded with strip emery paper of about 80 grit, like shining your shoes. You can also use open-screen-type sanding strips to clean the mill scale off the tubes. Flat sheets of 4130 steel can be sanded by hand block sanding the edges back to 1 inch from the edge to be welded. Use a piece of 80 to 120 grit emery paper and wrap it around a block of wood to make the sanding easier.

Just a few minutes prior to welding, clean the weld area of the tubes of sheet metal with acetone or denatured alcohol and a clean, white lint-free cloth to remove all grease and oil. Fingerprint oils contaminate welds, too. Clean the parts as thoroughly as if you were going to paint them. Do not expect the heat from welding to evaporate the dirt and oils.

Immediately prior to welding, clean the first two or three sticks of welding rod with acetone or denatured alcohol, using a clean, white lint-free cloth to wipe each stick of welding wire. From this point, do not touch the welding rod with your bare fingers or with dirty or oily gloves.

Every welding project begins with cutting the materials into the proper lengths. A cut-off saw like the one being used here by Mitch Matthews costs about $200 and will save lots of hacksaw work. *Richard Finch*

For nearly 75 years, filing fishmouth joints in tubular structures was the best way to ensure a good fit-up. Today, there is a better way to do this task. *Richard Finch*

WELDING CONDITIONS—WHERE TO DO THE WELDING

Do the welding in a clean, warm, well-lighted area that is free of wind or drafts from fans, opening doors, and open windows. Make sure that there are no liquid or solid combustibles in the welding area that could catch fire from sparks or arcs from your welding.

Welding in bright sunlight is far better than welding in a dark room. You can see the weld seam and the weld puddle better in good lighting conditions.

> # CAUTION
>
> Caution: Do not, under any circumstances, sand thin-wall tubing or thin sheet metal with a power sanding belt or disc, since power sanding would remove too much metal and severely weaken the metal in the welded zone. Hand sanding is the only safe way to remove mill scale and oxidation from metal to be welded.
>
> Sandblasting or glass-bead cleaning will safely clean off mill scale and oxidation, but the cleanup process to remove all the sand or glass dust from the part is not worth the time it takes. You absolutely do not want to weld your valuable parts if they are covered with sand dust and glass dust.
>
> Also, do not attempt to remove mill scale and oxidation with a power wire brush because the brush will imbed metal from its bristles into the metal to be welded, and this wire brush metal will contaminate your welds. Also, if the power wire brush is quite stiff, it will actually erode the parts to be welded and cause them to be weakened in the weld zone where you cleaned them.

Welds made in warm rooms, 80° to 95°F, are more likely to be good welds than those made in cold rooms. The parts you are welding should never be cold to your touch.

If you are welding parts that are 1/4-inch thick or thicker, you will have better luck if you preheat the parts to 250°F, and if the part is 1/2-inch thick or thicker, be sure to preheat it to 350°F in your kitchen oven for at least one hour before starting to weld. Try to block the part to be welded up off the steel of your welding table so the mass of the welding table will not pull the heat out of your weld assembly.

During and after welding, you may clean the weld area with a small stainless-steel wire brush. Do not brush the weld or the seam with a brush that has copper, brass, or aluminum bristles, because the non-compatible bristles will transfer metal to the weld and will eventually cause the weld to crack.

ADDITIONAL TIPS FOR CLEANING PARTS PRIOR TO WELDING

Liquid cleaning of the parts just prior to welding should also include acid cleaning if the parts are aluminum or slightly rusty steel. Acid cleaners are available from several sources, but paint stores are the easiest place to find them. Ask for a phosphoric acid solution. You may find it by trade names such as OSPO or Metal Prop. The cost will vary from $1.50 for one quart of phosphoric acid to $12.50 for a quart of name-brand metal cleaner. In most cases, you will need to dilute the phosphoric acid with water (4 to 10 parts water to 1 part acid) to remove rust and aluminum oxide from your parts. You can also find phosphoric acid in swimming-pool and spa supply stores because it is used to adjust water pH in pools and spas.

To clean aluminum parts prior to welding, prepare a mixture of phosphoric acid and water, and soak the parts in it for 30 minutes. Then remove the parts from the acid, rinse them in soft water, and allow them to air dry. Do not blow-dry the parts with compressed air, because most air compressors put oil into the air stream.

To clean rusty steel parts prior to welding, it's easy to mix up a three-to-one mixture of water and phosphoric acid (3 parts water to 1 part acid), put the mixture in a spray bottle, and spray the parts to dissolve the rust. After soaking for 30 minutes, rinse the parts in soft water. Any remaining rust will now sand or scrape off like old dried paint. The rust can also be wire brushed off in most instances.

IS THIS ALL A LOT OF WORK?

It takes a lot longer to read about how to do proper weld prep than it does to do it. On your next project, try doing a better preparation job and see if your welds look a lot better than ever before. Once you do this, you will find it easy the next time.

BEST GRADE WELDING RODS

The best rod costs only a little more than the paint you'll use to make your project look good. The best part is how much better your welds will be when you use vacuum-melted M.C.-grade welding rod.

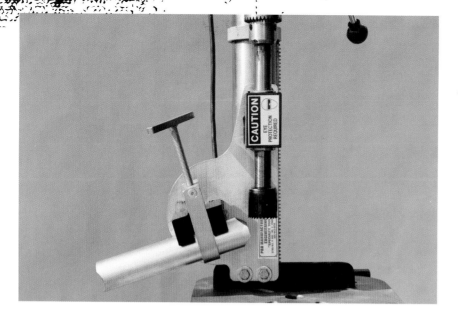

Hole-saw fishmouth tools can
accurately make tubular fit-ups in
just a fraction of the time it
takes to do the same job by hand.
Pro Tools

This fishmouth tool is mounted
on a workbench and operated with a
1/2-inch drill motor. It even
notches rectangular tubing, as seen
here. *Richard Finch*

ALTERNATE FITTING METHOD

If you plan to notch a lot of small tubing, say 3/8-, 1/2-, and 5/8-inch diameter, it would be more economical to adapt milling-machine end mills to your hole-saw joint-fitting fixture. When lubricated with cutting oil, an end mill will last for several hundred cuts, and it can be sharpened when it becomes dull.

A milling end-mill cutter takes a few seconds longer than a hole-saw cutter to produce a fishmouth fit on a given-size tube. This is because the hole saw cutter only has to cut a thin line through the tubing, while the end mill has to eat away a full circle of metal to cut through the tube.

The advantage to adapting an end mill to your joint-fitting fixture is that hole saws tend to shatter off all their teeth when cutting thin-wall small-diameter tubing. This does not happen when using an end mill cutter.

PLASMA CUTTING

Plasma cutting offers many advantages, especially compared with hand-hacksaw cutting, oxyacetylene torch cutting, and the high cost of making dies for stamping out small parts.

The big advantage to plasma cutting is that it cuts all metals with equal ease. Plasma will cut 3/16-inch and 1/4-inch stainless-steel plate into exhaust-pipe flanges just as easily as it will cut the same thickness mild-steel plate. And without changing settings, you can immediately cut 6061-T6 aluminum plate for welding special intake manifolds.

Stainless steel is one of the hardest common shop metals to cut. It is so resistant to cutting that it will dull an expensive, high-speed bi-metal hacksaw blade in just a few seconds. Then the new blade is just scrap.

Cutting stainless-steel plate or sheet, aluminum plate or sheet, 4130-steel plate or sheet, and even

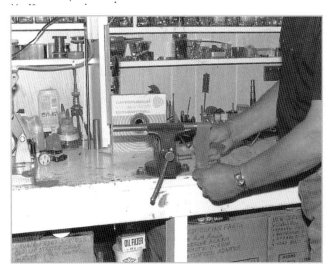

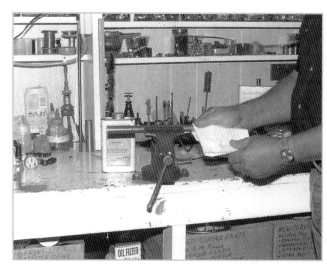

Every tube must be cleaned before welding. A strip of carborundum emery cloth is being used to sand the thin film of mill scale off a 3/4-inch x 0.032-inch chrome-moly tube. Every place that will be welded must be cleaned like this. *Richard Finch*

After the mill scale is sanded off the tube, acetone on a paper towel is used to remove all traces of oil and dust before the tube is welded. *Richard Finch*

brass and copper with plasma is almost as easy as drawing a line on the metal with a marking pen. But freehand plasma cutting often leaves a shaky cut line, so try to provide a guide for your cuts with a plasma cutter.

NUMERIC PLASMA CUTTERS

If you consider yourself to be in production, welding most of the day, every day, you should consider fitting your parts with a computer-controlled plasma-cutting setup. For many years it was possible to flame-cut shapes and flanges by having an optically guided pantograph torch or a gang of torches follow a line drawing on a piece of white paper. That was a major step forward in mass production, but recent developments make it possible to produce even better and faster cuts in all metals with numerically controlled automatic plasma-cutting machines. Talk to your welding equipment dealer if you need to increase your production and the quality of your parts.

This chapter contains photos of an operation in Hays, Kansas, that makes excellent use of CNC plasma cutting to produce net-size cuts in 4130 steel tubing.

BAND-SAW CUTTING

Any band saw that has a separate belt-driven drive wheel can be converted to cut steel and aluminum. The only band saws that could not be easily converted are model-makers' direct-drive saws.

If your band saw has a belt drive, you can substitute a compact speed-reduction unit that provides you with at least three or four different output speed ratios. This can be done by adding two extra jack shafts to the base that the electric motor mounts on. Then you add extra belts and chains.

The first ratio from the motor to the first jack shaft should be V-belt drive, probably a two-to-one reduction with a 2-inch pulley on the motor and a 4-inch pulley on the jack shaft. V-belts can slip under lots of torque, so you will probably want to use a no. 35 pitch chain on the final low-speed ratio.

BLADE SPEEDS

Because different brands of band saws have different diameters (and circumferences) of saw-blade drive wheels, you have to calculate (using shop math) the correct rpm to turn your band saw to obtain the correct blade speeds. Blade speeds are always expressed in fpm (feet of blade travel per minute). On the next page there is a common example of blade-speed calculation on a specific band saw. Using this, you can calculate the desired rpm numbers for your own band saw.

Let's say that your present band saw has a 1/3-hoursepower electric motor that turns 1,725 revolutions per minute and your band saw drive wheel is 10 inches in diameter (31.416 inches in circumference). Every time the drive wheel turns one revolution, the blade is traveling about 31 1/2 inches, or slightly

Bandsaw Blade Speeds Chart			
Material	**Matl. Number**	**Name**	**FeetPer-Minute**
Aluminum	6061	Weldable	1,200
Carbon Steel	1020	Mild Steel	330
Low Carbon Steel	4130	Chromemoly	270
Stainless Steel	308	Weldable	Not Recommended
Inconel	600	Weldable	70
Titanium	99 %	Pure	70
Titanium	Ti6Al4V	Weldable	45
Bronzes	Most Grades		180
Plywood	to 1/2-inch		2,400
Oak	to 4 inches		1,800

Chart information from American Saw and Manufacturing Company. Blade speeds must be accurate to avoid burning the blade.

Bandsaw Blade Teeth-Per-Inch Chart		
Material	**Thickness**	**Blade Teeth/Inch**
4130 Steel	0.20 to .100-inch	14
1020 Steel	0.50 to .125-inch	10
4130 Steel	.100 to 1.000-inch	10
6061 Steel	0.050 to .1250-inch	10
6061Steel	0.125 to 6.000-inch	9
3-Ply Plywood	0.063 to .250-inch	10
Solid Oak	1.000 to 4.000-inch	10
White Pain	.500 to 4.000-inch	6

Consult this chart for proper blade teeth. Half-inch wide blades are stronger than quarter-inch wide blades.

These two pieces of 7/8-inch x 0.032-inch tube are fitted perfectly, and the mill scale has been sanded off. Try to make every tubular joint fit like this. *Richard Finch*

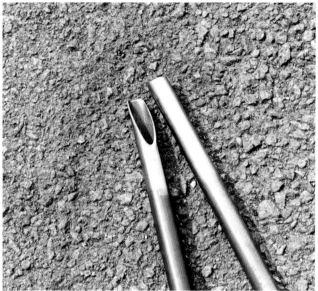

For angles greater than 45 degrees, some hand fitting still has to be done, as is shown on these two tubes for a race car suspension. *Richard Finch*

less than 3 feet per revolution. If your belt drive is a two-to-one unit, the band saw drive wheel is turning 863 revolutions per minute, and the blade is traveling 27,096 inches in one minute. Divide inches by 12 to obtain 2,258 feet per minute of blade travel, which is great for sawing thin plywood but way too fast to saw aluminum or steel.

You need to slow the blade down with another two-to-one reduction ratio to saw aluminum at 1,126 feet per minute, or another three-to-one ratio to saw steel at 375 feet per minute. You can calculate the reduction ratios you need to set up for your particular band saw. The bandsaw blade speeds chart gives blade speeds for metal.

BI-METAL BLADES
Always buy bi-metal band-saw blades. Single-metal blades wear out 100 times faster and never cut as well as bi-metal.

CLEANING OFF RUST
It is acceptable to use 4130 steel tubing that has a thin film of rust on it if the rust has not noticeably pitted the metal. In fact, most tubular frames will start to rust just an hour or two after they have been tack welded.

Tack-welded airplane fuselages and race car frames have been hauled cross-country after they were tack welded and before they were finish welded

The tube that angles up to the right in this photo has been poorly fitted. You can see the large gap that would surely be the cause of a crack in the weld if the tube is not replaced with one that fits properly. *Richard Finch*

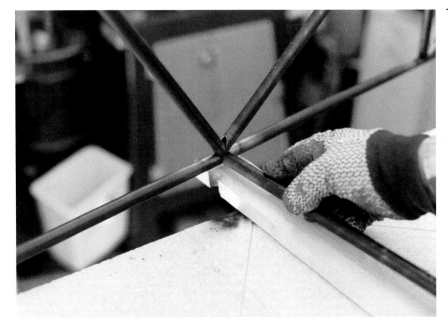

Mittler Brothers Machine and Tool makes this very heavy-duty tubing notcher that uses a milling cutter to notch the tubes for roll cages. *Richard Finch*

and painted. When you haul bare steel down the highway in the rain and fog, you can expect rust to form on it.

Before taking a tack-welded or otherwise-unpainted tubular structure out in the weather, coat it with a spray preservative that can be easily wiped off with solvent at a later time. Spray lubricants such as WD40 or LPS work well for temporary rust protection.

But if your tack-welded steel framework has already rusted slightly, the first thing to do is to wipe down the rust spots with a liquid metal prep that is ordinarily used in auto body shops for the same purpose. One brand that's easy to find in automotive parts stores is PP&G Metal Cleaner. It contains phos-

phoric acid, so wear rubber gloves and apply it with a small piece of cloth or a small sponge. When it dries to a white film, wipe the film off with a Scotchbrite pad, and you'll see that the rust is gone, too. A thick rust layer may take two or three applications. Next time, don't let your really good parts get rusty!

REASONS TO FIT PARTS CLOSELY

Assuming you were taught to weld thick parts for trailers and structural steel, you were probably taught to V-groove thicker pieces of metal so the weld would penetrate all the way through the base metal. You were taught correctly, but only for thick (over 0.090-inch wall thickness) metal. When you are

You will need to make lots of
weld-on tabs like these to attach
body panels, wiring harnesses,
fuel lines, and many other things to
your race car or airplane tubular
structure. *Richard Finch*

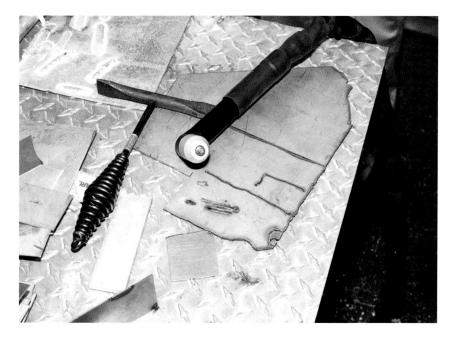

This plasma-cutter torch can cut
pencil-fine lines in anything
that is metallic, including aluminum
and even stainless steel. It is
the solution for cutting out
stainless-steel exhaust flanges from
1/4-inch-thick stainless plate.
Richard Finch

welding metal as thin as 0.005 inch to 0.049 inch, you should not have any space between the two or more parts.

The reason for tight fits on thin parts is that any air gap on the backside of the weld will allow for atmospheric contamination of the weld.

The front of the weld is protected by gas if TIG welding, by CO2 and argon if MIG welding, and by the combined oxyacetylene flame if gas welding. But nothing protects the backside of the weld if you have big, wide gaps. You can expect crystallized backsides if you try to bridge wide gaps.

When welding a tube cluster of 3/4-inch x 0.32-inch tubing, a good, tight fit protects the backside of the weld and prevents air from getting to it and contaminating it. Aluminum is less susceptible to contamination on the backside than steel is, but even aluminum welds usually look very lumpy if the fit-up of the parts was poor.

Another reason to try for good, tight fit-ups on thin metal is that the weld bead will be much easier to control and therefore much easier to make perfect.

High-tech airplane fabrication companies now use numerically controlled plasma cutters to precisely trim and fit even very small diameter 4130 steel tubing for use in airplane fuselage structures. *RANS, Inc./Richard Finch*

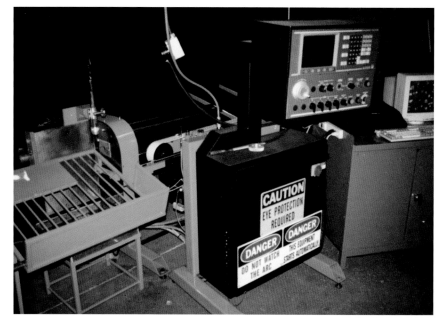

This custom-made plasma cutter is about ready to make a special fishmouth plasma cut on a stick of 1/2-inch diameter 4130 tubing. *RANS, Inc.*

Grouped by part number, 4130 steel tubing is used in airplane fuselage assemblies. *RANS, Inc.*

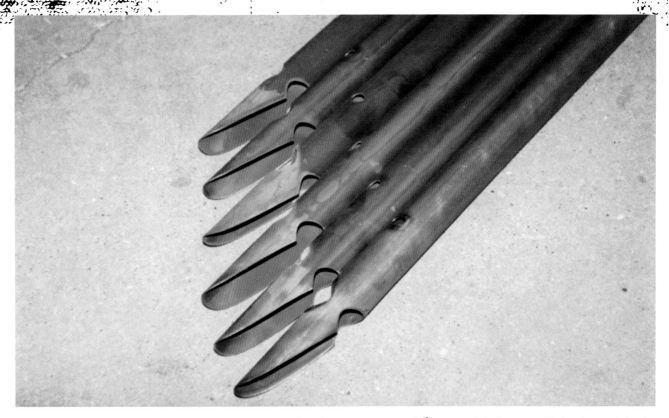

A close-up view of some intricate cuts made by the CNC plasma process in 7/8-inch x 0.032-inch wall thickness tubing. *RANS, Inc.*

A finished product is this S-7 Courier airplane. *RANS, Inc.*

A hole saw mounted in a drill press makes fast, accurate work of punching large holes in sheet steel. *Richard Finch*

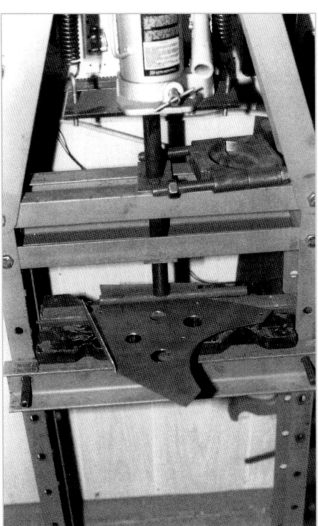

Smooth bends can be pressed into rather thick steel parts by using a hydraulic press, an angle frame, and a round steel bar, as you see here. *Richard Finch*

CHAPTER
4

JIGGING

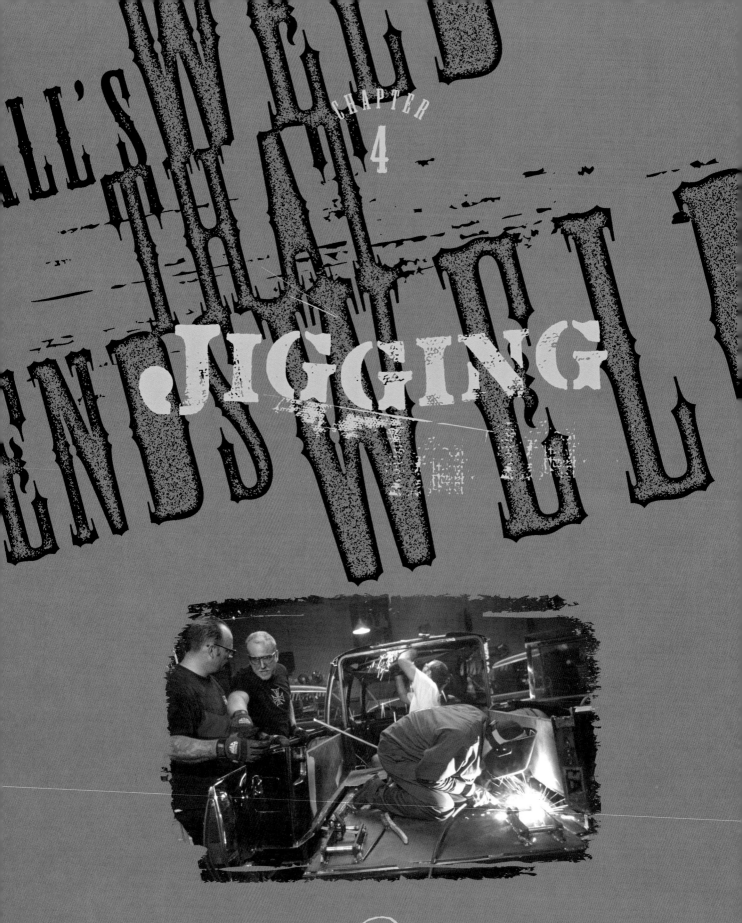

In the manufacturing and production business, the jigs that the parts are welded in are usually much heavier and more complex than the parts they produce. When you fabricate several units of a specific framework or assembly, a strong, intricate welding jig can significantly save time and materials.

If you are only making one or two units of a welded assembly, you can usually get by with a temporary lightweight jig. A pair of Vise-Grip pliers will often suffice, and several C-clamps are often the best way to clamp things together for welding. In this chapter, you will be shown several ways to jig parts together for welding. Then you can decide which of the pictured jigs will best suit your project.

WELD TABLE JIGS

You've probably noticed the artistic, polished-stainless-steel boat railings on pleasure yachts and even some ski boats. One particular shop in Santa Barbara, California, designs boat railings for each individual boat and then fabricates the railings on a 4x8-foot welding table made of 3/8-inch steel plate.

It's easy to draw a layout on the top of a welding table with a black marker. After the layout and job are finished, the marker lines and notes can be removed with acetone.

Since each boat railing is unique, it would be too time consuming and expensive to build a welding jig for each one. Instead, the stainless-steel railing base plates are tack welded to the tabletop, and the polished tubing (usually 1-inch o.d. x 0.065-inch wall) is then formed, trimmed, and welded to each base plate.

After the railings are completely welded, the new railing is taken out to the harbor and bolted to the deck of the yacht. The base-plate tack welds are cut off the welding tabletop with an abrasive cut-off wheel, the tack-weld spot is ground and polished smooth.

The tack welds on the welding tabletop are then ground away with a 4-inch hand grinder equipped with an 80-grit flap wheel. Next, the table is wiped down with acetone and prepared for the next boat-railing job. The temporary welding jig served its purpose and can be changed to fit any size and shape of boat deck.

PLYWOOD JIGS

For many years, probably since the first steel-tube-fuselage airplane was built, welders have been building fuselage structures on plywood tabletops. This method is similar to the way that a stick-and-

paper balsa flying model is built, except the framework on the model is glued rather than welded.

Take a look at the photos in this chapter and also the photos in Chapter 9, "Gas Welding Steel and Stainless Steel," to see how an airplane welding table is built. You will have to adjust the length and width of your plywood or particleboard welding table to suit your project, but the basic design will be the same.

Be sure that the height of the table is right so you'll have an easy stand-up welding layout. Kitchen cabinet work tops are designed for stand-up food preparation, so measure your kitchen cabinet-top height and make your plywood or particleboard table the same height.

After the table is built, you will need to level it for ease of measuring and setting up the tubular structure. Small, tapered wood shims can be used to level the base of the table to the floor. A hot glue gun or Bondo will hold the tapered shims in place on the floor.

Even if you plan to TIG or MIG weld your fuselage structure, the plywood or particleboard tabletop will work well. To make electrical contact with your framework, simply clip the welding-machine ground clamp to one of the main longerons or other part that will carry the welding current.

Don't spend too much time and money on plywood or particle board welding tables unless you plan to build several parts to the same set of plans. Then you might take a little extra time to make the table more user-friendly.

CRUDE WELD TABLES

Take a look at the simple plywood welding table in chapter 9 that is merely a piece of 1/2-inch plywood resting on a bunch of rubber traffic cones. For a one-of-a-kind race car frame, a crude-but-effective plywood welding table proved to be completely adequate. You could make use of a similar welding table if you need to.

PERMANENT WELDING JIGS

No magic number of welded assemblies can dictate when it is economical and useful to build a permanent welding jig. The answer usually depends on the total time spent fitting and welding and the level of accuracy and interchangeability needed.

If you were building freeform metal sculptures for wall decorations, you probably wouldn't need a welding jig. But if you are building aircraft landing-gear legs to be stocked as spares, you would definitely want the landing gear to be a bolt-in fit every time.

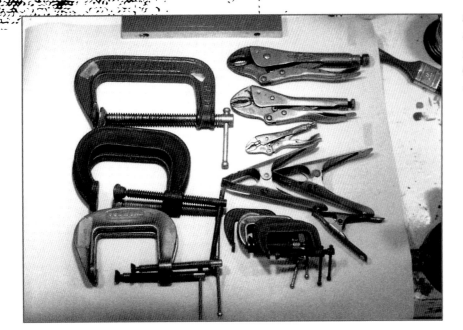

In this case, a simple but accurate welding jig would be a wise idea. Take a look at the airplane landing-gear welding jig in this chapter for one suggestion on building a simple but permanent welding jig.

In situations where speed and efficiency equal profit, steel-framework welding jigs are a necessity. The two airplane-part jigs shown in this chapter make it relatively simple to weld up a complete fuselage in the jig, with assurance that the next 10 and the next 100 welded assemblies will all be identical and that the associated parts will bolt together without the need to file or drill anything.

Heavyweight welding jigs are not always the best solution. It is a fact that a 2x4-foot-by 1/2-inch solid steel plate can flex several thousandths of an inch with

very little pressure. This means that welding up a tubular assembly that is simply bolted to the solid steel plate could still be able to twist or bend the plate as the tube structure is welded. If you are trying to maintain a few thousandths of an inch of fit-up toler-ance, the solid steel plate would not be rigid enough.

The best steel-welding jigs are light enough to be disassembled easily and are triangulated properly to prevent movement of the rig during welding. Bolt-together and pin-together welding jigs work well in most cases.

A perfect example of a very-high-production automobile that was jig-welded was the production run of the Pontiac Fiero sports car. To ensure perfect body-panel alignment, the body-mount pads on the

William's Lo-Buck Tools makes this adjustable alignment tool that works great for many tubing and even-angle stock fit-ups. *Richard Finch*

This aluminum angle-welding jig was used to build several identical landing-gear legs for a seaplane. *Richard Finch*

Fiero frame were all thicker than necessary at weld-up time. So when the space-frame chassis cooled after welding, automatic milling machines trimmed all the body-mount pads to the perfect height. In this particular auto-building technology, the fit of the plastic body panels was considered of major importance.

DESIGNING A WELDING JIG

Often it is easier to build the first part to the dimensions on the plans and then simply make a jig to fit the first actual part. This is the design method used by many engineers who design welding jigs.

Another way to design a welding jig is to first cut out all the necessary parts from metal, fit them together, and then build a jig that will hold all the parts

in place while they are welded. If the welded assembly is not too complicated, this method works pretty well.

Still another way to make a welding jig to fit a large structure, such as an airplane fuselage, is to design the welding jig from the blueprint that defines the fuselage. In one such case, a rotatable welding jig that defined the size and shape of the fuselage structure and at the same time provided a weld fixture for a fuselage that measured 16 feet long, 4 feet wide, and 4 feet high.

That particular welding jig began with a 2 1/2-inch-diameter, 0.080-inch wall tube, 20 feet long. At specific inch station locations along the length of the 2 1/2-inch tube, fuselage bulkhead brackets were located. Then the bulkheads were attached to the

After the Osprey II landing gear leg was welded in the jig, it was sandblasted and powder coated to prevent rust when landing in the water. *Richard Finch*

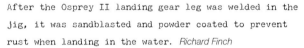

This particleboard and white pine welding jig ensures proper alignment when welding up the sides for a Finchbird experimental airplane. *Richard Finch*

An excellent fit-up of 4130 steel tubing members is evident in this photo. TIG or MIG welding can be done on this particleboard weld jig by clamping the ground to one of the tubes. *Richard Finch*

brackets, and the longeron tubes were fitted to the bulkhead and tack-welded in place.

As the fuselage assembly progressed, the 2 1/2-inch tube provided a center point that allowed the fuselage structure to be rotated for ease of welding. As you likely know, the easiest and best welds are made flat, not uphill, not overhead, and not upside down. And, of course, the 2 1/2-inch tube rotated in sawhorse-type frames at each end.

IDEAS FOR JIGS

Take a close look at the numerous welding jigs in this chapter and elsewhere in the book for ideas on how to design your particular welding jigs. There is no single, perfect way to design a welding jig. The second and third jigs you design will probably be better than your first.

After one side of the airplane
fuselage was tack welded with a
gas-welding torch, the frame was
removed from the jig so the second
side could be built on the jig.
Richard Finch

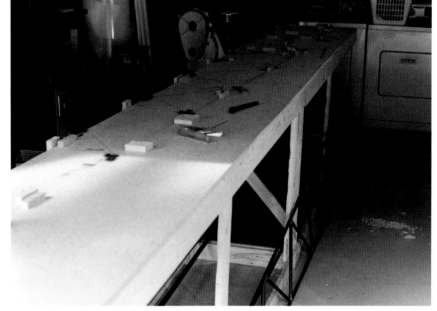

A typical aircraft weld repair shop.
Wag-Aero Group

A tack-welded 4130 steel-tubing
airplane fuselage has been removed
from its alignment jig for shipment
to a customer, who will complete the
welding on the tack welds, thereby
saving several thousands of dollars
in welding labor. *Wag-Aero Group*

An aircraft welder is shown TIG
welding a subassembly
on a square-tube welding jig that
ensures identical parts every time.
RANS, Inc.

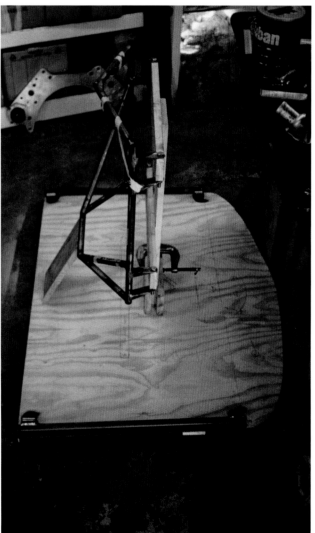

This engine-mount welding jig was designed around the
shape and actual size of the airplane firewall. Steel
brackets locate the firewall mounting points.
Richard Finch

This light but rigid and strong welding jig ensures that every airplane fuselage built in this jig will be identical to the others. The jig is made from thin-wall square tubing. *RANS, Inc.*

A completed and painted airplane fuselage frame built in the welding jig shown in the left photo. *RANS, Inc.*

In order to ensure that dozens of Chevrolet V-6 engine mounts will fit on RV-6A kit airplanes, a welder builds each mount in this simple but strong angle-iron welding jig. *Belted Air Power*

CHAPTER 5

TIG welding

4130 STEEL TUBING

Like the journey of 1,000 miles that begins with one step, TIG welding 4130 steel tubing begins with starting the arc, making a very small molten puddle, adding one dip of welding rod to the puddle, then pulling the rod out of the heat of the arc. If you do this arc-welding process four or five times, you have made a tack weld. If you have done this welding process 15 or 20 times, you have welded halfway around a tubular joint. Repeating the process thousands of times means that your journey is complete. You have assembled a tubular frame by TIG welding it.

PREHEATING?

Here's another old wives tale (old welders tale?) that's still passed on by word of mouth: Chrome-moly assemblies must be preheated by subjecting them to the flame of an oxyacetylene gas torch just before you begin welding them. This is simply incorrect.

Doing this is one more way to damage your 4130 steel (chrome-moly) structure. First of all, the experts say that preheating is not necessary for 4130 steel under 1/4-inch thickness. The next reason to avoid torch-heating 4130 steel is that you really don't know what temperature it is heated to if you are just passing a flame over it. It could be anywhere between 100° and 1,000°F, which is no way to preheat for welding. The next reason for not preheating your tubular 4130 steel structure is that it would be cooled back to ambient temperature before you could complete the first 20 percent of the welds. You gain nothing by preheating a tubular structure before welding, and you take the chance of harming it by applying an open-air flame.

It is certainly not a wise idea to weld a 4130 steel structure in a freezing workshop in the winter. Your welding workshop should be shirt-sleeve comfortable, with a room temperature of 75° to 95°F, even in winter. If it isn't, buy a heater. It is hard on metal to weld it if the metal is cold.

FITTING AND CLEANING

Read Chapter 3 again, and pay special attention to what it says about fitting parts tightly. A watertight or a daylight-tight fit is a lot easier to weld than a loose fit where you can see a big gap between the parts. Make sure you have cleaned the area that will be affected by the heat of the weld, and be sure to clean the welding rod. Most things that you will TIG weld will be critical components in machinery that protects human life. For example, an airplane's engine mount is a very critical structure because it holds the engine in an airplane. The front suspension of a race car is equally important when the car is traveling at 200 miles per hour.

TIG WELDING PROCEDURE

Let's say that you are welding a tubing cluster of 7/8-inch o.d. x 0.049-inch wall 4130-N steel. Here is a good setup:

- Water-cooled torch, WP-10 size.
- No. 8 ceramic cup.
- 1/16-inch diameter, 2 percent thoriated tungsten.
- Argon gas, set to 20 cfh.
- Pre-flow timer set to 0.5 second.
- Post-flow timer set to 10 seconds.
- Amps set to 75, percent set to 75.
- Polarity set to DC straight (DCSP).
- High frequency set to start only.
- Tungsten ground to pencil-point shape.
- Tungsten stick out 1/8 inch.
- Foot pedal ready to operate to start the arc.

The setup listed above is for the old standby welding machine. If you have a newer square-wave TIG-welding machine, you have several additional options. You will be able to dial in a known "best setup" and you can also dial in a "crater-fill" option. Or you can use the top-of-the-line welding machines just like you would an old standby welding machine.

TORCH CUP SIZES

The optimum ceramic cup size for most steel and stainless steel welding is a No. 8, because that size provides good argon flow for proper weld coverage, but it also allows you a good, unobstructed view of the weld puddle. When you're welding tubing, there will be tight corners that a No. 8 ceramic cup will not fit into. In this situation, temporarily switch to a No. 6 or even a No. 4 cup, but be sure to go back to a No. 8 or a No. 10 cup as soon as access to the weld seam permits.

The problem with small cup sizes is that they do not distribute the 20 cfh argon flow as well as larger cups do, and you will have problems with air-contaminated welds, which are caused by using a cup that is too small.

TUNGSTEN STICK-OUT

Ideally, the tungsten should always be completely inside the argon gas flowing out of the cup. Yes, it is possible to extend the tungsten out of the cup by 1/2 inch or more, but it will often become contaminated

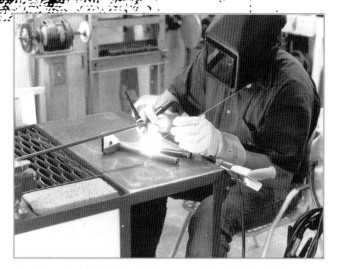

In this, two 4130 steel tubes are being TIG welded together for a turbocharger bracket. The operator is using new, clean, lightweight gloves made specifically for Heliarc welding. *Richard Finch*

This is the backside of a 300-horsepower, twin-turbocharged engine. In this photo you can see the TIG-welded 4130 steel engine mount that was *not* stress-relieved after it was welded. Not a single one of more than 1,600 identical engine mounts were stress-relieved, and not one ever cracked in use. Also note the intricately welded stainless-steel exhaust system. *Richard Finch*

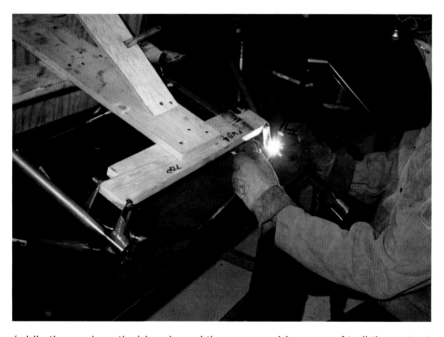

TIG-welding a 4130 steel engine mount, jigged up in a wooden jig. The engine mount was not stress-relieved after it was welded, and it fit the airplane and Buick V-6 engine perfectly. *Richard Finch*

(while the arc is active) by air, and then your weld instantly becomes contaminated.

The best procedure is to extend the tungsten past the cup by no more than one-half the width of the cup. If the cup is 1/2-inch across, let the tungsten stick out no more than 1/4 inch.

There will be corners to weld where a No. 4 cup is required to gain access, and you may need to let the tungsten stick out of the cup by up to 1/2 inch, but when you do that, you will be taking a big chance on contaminating the tungsten either by touching it with the welding rod or by touching the weld puddle with it.

At all times, try to make a No. 8 cup and a 1/16-inch tungsten work.

STRESS-RELIEVING AFTER ARC WELDING

Right up front, you should know that it is not possible to accurately stress-relieve a welded 4130 steel assembly by heating it red-hot with an oxyacetylene torch in an open-air (or closed-air) workshop.

Stress-relieving a welded 4130 steel assembly such as an aircraft engine mount or a race car rear suspension member is a metallurgical process that

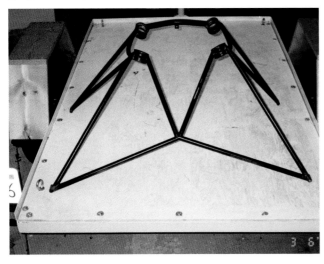

This is a typical Lycoming engine mount. The mount was not stress-relieved after welding, and no cracks developed in over 1,600 hours of operation. *Richard Finch*

The white tubular frame in this photo is a TIG-welded 4130 steel engine mount used in a Helio Courier STOL airplane. *Richard Finch*

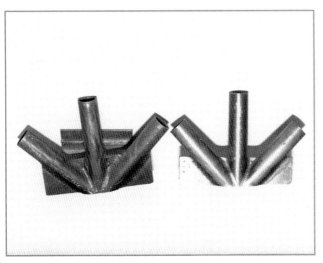

These two welded tube clusters are both certified aircraft welding coupons that have passed certification inspection. If your welds can match these, you will probably be a good aircraft welder. *Richard Finch*

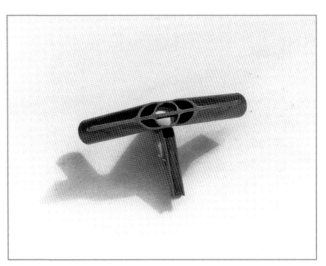

This end view of an aircraft certification cluster shows at least 100 percent weld penetration and a flawless fit-up of the tubes to the plate. *Richard Finch*

requires at least six hours to do correctly. The steel grain structure must be slowly brought up to about 1,150°F, held at that temperature for several minutes to a couple of hours, then slowly cooled back to room temperature. This very specific process absolutely cannot be accomplished by a hand-held torch in a welding shop.

ENGINE MOUNTS

At an aircraft factory over 800 airplanes were built in eight years. Each twin-engine airplane had two engine mounts, so over 1,600 TIG-welded 4130 steel mounts

were built. Not a single one of those 1,600 mounts was stress-relieved after welding. According to FAA and AOPA records, not one single engine mount has ever failed in service!

Even when a propeller blade came loose and caused the engine to tear out of the wing, the welds on the engine mount held. Magnaflux inspections were conducted on every engine mount for cracks and porosity after welding, and none of the 1,600 engine mounts failed.

The engine mounts were made from 4130-N steel tubing, welded with DCSP (DC straight polarity) TIG

This tubular square frame was TIG welded, then sawed through on the lower tube without stress relieving. The very slight mismatch in the lower tube shows that almost no stresses were caused by the TIG welding. In most situations, post-weld stress-relieving attempts can harm the structure far more than they will help it. *Richard Finch*

A close-up of the TIG welds on this 4-cylinder LOM aircraft engine in an RV-4 kitplane lets you see the kind of welds to try for. Good workmanship is exhibited here. *Richard Finch*

The diameter of the welding rod, the diameter of the tungsten electrode, and the close fit-up of parts contributed to this very small and neat weld on a PT-6 engine mount. *Richard Finch*

An Alaskan bush plane landing-gear and brake-caliper mounting plate shows the possibilities of unique engineering designs made possible by the use of TIG welding. *Richard Finch*

welding, using high-quality certified 4130 steel welding rod, 1/16-inch diameter, base, not copper coated. Special care was taken to ensure good fit-ups of the tubing, and all the mount tubes were cleaned with acetone before welding.

After welding, each mount was glass-bead cleaned and magnafluxed. Next, each mount was filled with an oil-based preservative called Braycoat, allowed to drain, and then the oil holes were plugged with pop rivets. The mounts were painted with green zinc chromate primer and then painted with silver epoxy paint. If you process your tubular 4130

steel-welded assemblies in the same way, you should have zero defects, too!

TUNGSTEN DIAMETERS

Two percent thoriated tungsten for welding steel and stainless steel comes in sizes that range from a tiny 0.020-inch to a big 3/16-inch diameter. A good rule of thumb is to use a tungsten diameter that's about the same as the thickness of the steel part you're welding. If you're welding 0.049 inch wall thickness 4130 steel, you would want a 1/16-inch-diameter tungsten electrode (0.063-inch diameter).

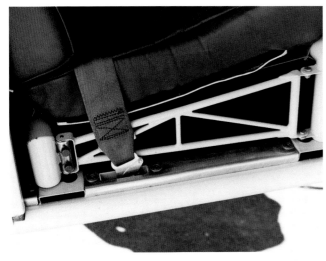

A close-up of the rear seat structure of the Alaska bush plane shows the very lightweight but strong TIG-welded frame. *Richard Finch*

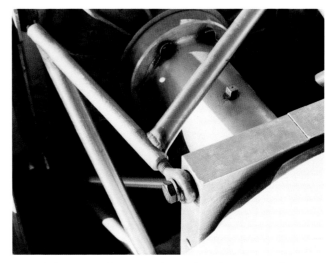

This E-Racer airplane uses TIG-welded braces to align and retain its rear propeller bearing housing. *Richard Finch*

A TIG tack weld consists of about three drops (dabs) of 4130 welding rod to hold the tube to the rectangular member for fit-checking before complete welding. *Richard Finch*

This race car has a very spindly but strong TIG-welded 4130 steel front suspension. It is chrome plated and baked to normalize after the hydrogen embrittlement chrome plating is done. *Richard Finch*

Inch-Decimal Wire Size Conversions

.020-inch	(0.5 mm)
.040-inch	(1.0 mm)
1/16-inch	(1.6 mm)
3/32-inch	(2.4 mm)
1/8-inch	(3.2 mm)
5/32-inch	(4.0 mm)
3/16-inch	(4.8 mm)

Chart information from American Saw and Manufacturing Company.
Blade speeds must be accurate to avoid burning the blade.

If you are welding 0.032-inch wall thickness tubing, use a 0.040-inch-diameter tungsten. You should have the following diameters of tungsten, collets, and chucks in your tungsten tray:

TUNGSTEN LENGTHS

Standard tungsten lengths are 7 inches and 3 1/2 inches. It is less expensive to buy the 7-inch length and grind them in half for use with medium or short back caps. Using the full 7-inch-long tungsten with a long torch back cap is unhandy, and the long back cap can get in your way. Avoid using the long back cap as much as possible.

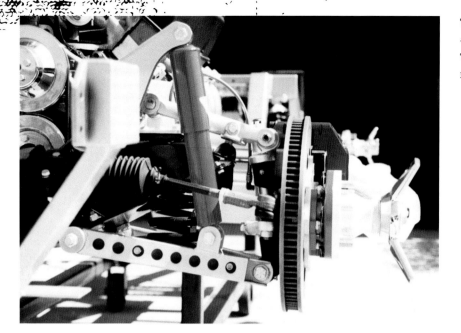

TIG welds on the lower A-arm suspensions of replica cars. After TIG welding, the A-arms are cadmium plated to prevent rust. *Richard Finch*

This roll-cage structure on a Bonneville record-holder race car is TIG-welded because TIG welding is the most accurate and sound of all forms of manual welding. *Richard Finch*

GRINDING TUNGSTEN POINTS

There are two basic point shapes for all TIG welding, including aluminum welding. Use a pencil-point-shape tungsten for steel and a crayon shape for aluminum.

The method you use to grind your tungsten points will directly affect the shape and control of your TIG arc. A crooked tip will give you a crooked arc. Often, the arc will even come off the side of the tungsten with a misshapen tip. Tungsten tips ground radially will encourage the arc to travel around in circles, following the circular grind marks on the tip.

The best tip on the tungsten is a perfect cone shape with no grinding marks. One company, listed in Appendix A, furnishes diamond-ground tungsten, polished to 6 to 8 root mean square, compared to 75

root mean square for typical hand-ground tungsten.

Most good welding shops reserve a special 400-grit grinding wheel for tungsten only. You don't want to grind other metals on the same wheel that your tungsten is ground on because steel from other grinding will adhere to the tungsten and contaminate it. Properly grinding your tungsten is just one of the many precautions you must observe in order to get high-quality welds.

TIG TORCH WATER CABLES

If you are reasonably careful and don't drag your torch cables over hot, just-welded places, you can weld for many months without ever scorching or melting holes in your TIG cables.

Mooney Aircraft fabricates nose
landing-gear assemblies and main
landing-gear assemblies by TIG
welding 4130 steel tubing and 3/16-
inch 4130 steel plate. *Richard Finch*

A welder TIG welds a bracket to an
airplane fuselage. *RANS, Inc.*

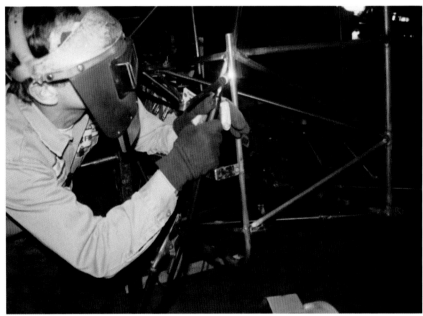

The worst thing you can do with your cables is to cover them with a heavy leather shield that zips or snaps shut. The weight and stiffness of leather or fabric cable shields will affect the accuracy and quality of your welds. The lighter the weight of your TIG torch and its associated lines, the less fatigue you will experience while welding. Guiding a torch and cables that weigh just a few ounces is far easier than trying to guide a torch and leather-covered cables that weigh several pounds.

TIG TORCH SIZES

For aircraft and race car welding, you should have a very compact water-cooled torch that will accept 0.375-inch diameter chucks and ceramic cups. Large heavy-duty air- and water-cooled torches are for nuclear power plant and oil refinery pipe welding. This is another situation where one tool (torch) should not be expected to do all jobs. You may decide to have two or even three different TIG torches in your welding tool cabinet.

The only reason for owning an air-cooled TIG torch is so you could do field repairs where water tanks or water-cooling radiators would not be easy to set up. In almost every case, a water-cooled torch works better than an air-cooled torch. Chapter 2 tells about the best torches to buy.

VACUUM-CHAMBER TIG WELDING

As already stated, stainless steel and titanium require protection for the backside of the weld bead to prevent "sugar," or crystallization of the back of the

Dozens of airplane fuselage frames
are completed at an airplane factory
in Hays, Kansas. *RANS, Inc.*

At least 50 separate pieces of
number 308 stainless steel were used
to weld the lower inlet shape on
this Turbo Tracker S-2 nose cowl.
Just barely visible under the prop
spinner area is a secondary heated
inlet that was considered impossible
to fabricate. *Richard Finch*

Practice your TIG stainless steel
welding skills by butt-welding two
pieces together like this, but argon
purge the back side of the weld
to prevent "sugar" in the weld.
Richard Finch

The almost-invisible weld seam on this blown small-block Chevrolet dragster exhaust is the result of: (1) a very good fit-up, (2) argon purge behind the weld, (3) .040-inch weld rod, and (4) a welder who took time to make his or her welds look good. *Richard Finch*

Properties of Steel vs. Temperature

Temperature	Process or Condition	Color
2,900°F		
2,800°F		
2,700°F		
2,600°F	Liquid State	Melts
2,500°F		
2,400°F		
2,300°F		
2,200°F		
2,100°F	Forging-Hot Working	White
2,000°F		
1,900°F	Magnetism Is Lost	Bright Yellow
1,800°F	Carburizing	Lemon
1,700°F	Annealing	Orange
1,600°F	Normalizing	Salmon
1,500°F	Atomic Changes	Bright Red
1,400°F		
1,300°F		Cherry Red
1,200°F	Atomic Changes	Blood
1,100°F	Stress Relieving	Red
1,000°F	Nitriding	Faint Red
900°F		
800°F		
700°F		
600°F		
500°F		
400°F		Black
300°F	Preheating For Welding	
200°F		
100°F		
0°F		

Information courtesy of *Air Liquide America, L.P*

A race shop in California TIG welded this beautiful chrome-plated mild-steel exhaust system on one of its cars. No backside argon purging is required when welding mild-steel tubing. *Butler Racing, Inc.*

Pieces of straight and 180° curved stainless-steel pipe were trimmed to fit and butt welded to make the exhaust for this V-6-powered race car. *Richard Finch*

A thumb-button-operated TIG torch issued on a couple of stainless-steel plates. No foot control is needed with this arrangement. *Richard Finch*

Every part of the front suspension on this dragster right front wheel is TIG welded for maximum strength. because it is a one-of-a-kind suspension. Vacuum oven stress relief was done after welding. *Richard Finch*

A TIG welder makes a repair on a stainless-steel aircraft muffler. He should be wearing gloves to protect his hands from the TIG welding's UV radiation. *Wag-Aero Group*

We are looking through the observation port in a vacuum chamber used for TIG welding stainless steel and titanium parts without atmospheric contaminants.
Vacuum Atmospheres Company

weld bead. This is an easy thing to do when you're welding an exhaust manifold or a small oil or water tank where you can purge the backside of the weld by simply flowing 10 to 20 cubic feet of argon per hour to the weld area.

But when you are welding larger sheet-metal assemblies such as the Grumman S-2 Turbo Tracker nose cowling shown in this chapter, a vacuum chamber is the only way to ensure sugar-free welds that will not crack after welding.

Vacuum-chamber welding is something of a misnomer. The air (oxygen, hydrogen, and other impurities) is evacuated from the weld chamber, and the bad air is replaced with pure argon, making a completely inert atmosphere. To conserve argon, you would put several parts into the chamber at a time so you could weld them with only one evacuation and argon filling.

A good vacuum-welding chamber can be made to operate at less than 1 part per million each of O2 (oxygen), H2O (water), and N2 (nitrogen), and less than 20 parts per million of H2 (hydrogen). If your stainless-steel or titanium welds require better back-gas purging, consider using a vacuum chamber.

STRESS RELIEVING AFTER WELDING

One of the most repeated and most taught mistakes in aircraft welding is that each welded assembly must be stress-relieved after welding by reheating the welded area to blood red by heating it with an oxyacetylene torch, a process that usually takes less than two minutes to complete.

This quick reheating process actually does far more damage to the welded tubular structure than it ever does good. The metallurgically correct procedure for stress relieving a welded assembly, such as an aircraft engine mount, is described below:

First, a suitable, heavy, corrosion-proof fixture must be built to support the welded engine mount while it is oven-heated to blood red, so the mount will not twist and warp.

Next, the mount and its supporting fixture must be put into a vacuum oven for a four- to six-hour heating and cooling process.

The temperature of the oven is slowly brought up to about 1,250°F, taking about four hours to heat the mount from room temperature to the temperature where the metallic grain structure changes to fully relieve stresses. The temperature is held at this point for several minutes to an hour to ensure total relaxation of the metal grain structure.

Next, the heat is removed from the oven, and the engine-mount structure is allowed to cool naturally in a still-air condition, preferably in the vacuum of the oven.

Any attempt to speed up this process will result in possible hardening of the structure, crystallization of the weld area, and the inducing of cracks in the heated area.

This vacuum welding chamber makes it easy to get contamination-free welds on stainless-steel and titanium parts. The chamber is filled with low-pressure argon gas after the atmosphere is pumped out of the tank. *Vacuum Atmospheres Company*

PRE- AND POST-PURGE

There is a very good reason for the pre- and post-purge settings on a good TIG welding machine. The pre-purge of about 0.5 second is to ensure that argon gas will cover the weld area when the arc starts. Otherwise, there would be immediate contamination of the weld and the tungsten when the weld begins. If your welding machine does not have a pre-purge setting, hit the pedal and start the argon flowing for a second before you strike the arc.

After you finish the weld, do not immediately remove the torch from the weld. Hold the torch over the cooling weld for a count of 5 to 10 seconds to allow the argon post flow to cool and protect the weld until it cools below the critical contamination temperature. On clean steel and stainless steel, you can actually see the argon protecting the weld by not letting it change colors as it cools.

SCALING

Another noteworthy side effect of torch-heating welded tubular or plate structure another time after the initial weld has been completed is the obvious scaling and flaking on the surface of the 4130 steel. What this means in terms of strength is that a thin layer of the metal has been removed by the second heating process. This means that your 0.032-inch wall thickness tubing is now only 0.029 inch or even less because you caused a thin layer of the tubing to evaporate when you heated it again.

TEMPERATURE CONTROL

In order to correctly stress-relieve a welded 4130 steel thin-wall tubing assembly, a very narrow temperature range must be reached and held for several minutes. This temperature is usually 1,125° to 1,265°F, a range that is virtually impossible to attain with a hand-held oxyacetylene torch.

To quote the chart provided by the Tempil Division of Air Liquide America, L.P.: "Stress Relieving consists of heating to a point below the lower transformation temperature, then holding for a sufficiently long period to relieve locked-up stresses, then slowly cooling." Stress relieving is a very accurate process.

CHAPTER
6

TIG welding
ALUMINUM and
MAGNESIUM

Once you get the hang of it, TIG welding aluminum becomes the easiest of all welding processes. You just have to observe some rules.

The main difference between welding aluminum and welding steel is that steel changes color as it heats up to its melting point. But aluminum does not change color as it heats to its melting point.

As it's being heated, aluminum gets slightly duller than when it's at room temperature, then it starts to get shiny, and then very quickly, a molten puddle forms where the heat is being applied. But more about that later in this chapter. Now, you should determine the kind of welding equipment you need to do aluminum TIG welding.

TIG EQUIPMENT FOR ALUMINUM

It makes almost no sense to have a TIG welder that will not weld aluminum. You must have a welding machine that has AC current plus high frequency, or a machine that has square-wave AC capabilities. You cannot weld aluminum and magnesium with a DC-only machine. The reason that AC current is required for welding aluminum is that aluminum and magnesium naturally contain oxides that cannot be cleaned off by DC welding. The sine-wave characteristics of AC plus high frequency greatly aid in keeping the oxides from contaminating the weld puddle.

Read Chapter 2, "Shopping for Welding Equipment," to find the best TIG welder for aluminum. The right welder will make aluminum welding a very easy task.

CLEAN THE PARTS

One of the secrets to making really pretty welds in aluminum and magnesium is to clean and fit the parts properly. But if you use a sanding disc to clean the parts, you will imbed small particles of sanding-disc material into the surface to be welded. These small particles will contaminate your welds. And if you use a power wire brush to clean the parts, the steel bristles in the wire brush will erode off into the aluminum or magnesium and cause contamination in your welds. There are at least two solutions to the cleaning problem, caustic and plastic.

CAUSTIC CLEANERS

Easy places to find metal cleaners are automotive body, paint supply, and commercial paint stores. Ask for liquid cleaners, not paste. You want cleaners that will rinse off with water.

SCRUB PADS

The best thing to use to clean aluminum for welding is a Scotchbrite pad. The regular kitchen pot scouring pads work pretty well, and now 3M offers a pad that clips on a circular wheel that can be operated by an air angle grinder motor or even a 1/4-inch drill motor. These plastic-based scouring pads effectively clean surface oxides from aluminum and magnesium before welding. And be sure to degrease the parts by wiping them down with acetone just before welding.

ALUMINUM HEAT TRANSFER

Aluminum soaks up torch heat a lot faster than steel does, which means that you have to start off a little hotter (more amps) when you are TIG welding. In fact, it's even a good idea to use the next-diameter-larger tungsten electrode when TIG welding aluminum compared to the tungsten diameter you use for welding steel.

The result of a too-small-diameter tungsten is that under high heat, the tungsten will often splinter, and sometimes it will even break off while you're welding. So start with a tungsten one diameter larger than you would use if you were TIG welding steel.

Because aluminum transfers heat more efficiently than other metals, expect the entire part to get hotter than a steel part would. It's not a problem, and it's good to know that this is normal.

ALUMINUM ARCING

Aluminum is notably less conductive electrically than steel. This means that your aluminum part will tend to arc where it rests on the grounded steel welding table. The result of this will be noticeable pitting and burning of the aluminum where it touches the weld table.

The best way to prevent this arcing and burning is to provide a positive ground for the aluminum part in addition to where it rests on the table—usually a "welder's finger," a steel rod that rests on the welding table and on the part to be welded. The metal finger should have some weight to it to provide stability and to make a clamping-type electrical connection. Make several welder's fingers out of 3/8-inch and 1/2-inch-diameter steel rod. Just don't let your aluminum parts arc on the welding table while you're welding.

BALLING TUNGSTEN

In welding school, the teacher traditionally informs the class to purposely ball the tip of the pure (not thoriated) tungsten before making aluminum welds.

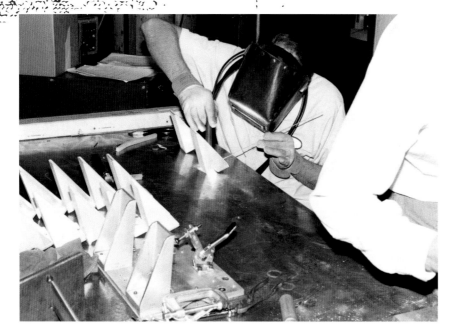

This is done by first setting the welding machine to DC and positive polarity, striking an arc on scrap aluminum or copper, and holding the arc until the tungsten tip melts from a crayon shape into a round, shiny ball shape. The teacher will tell you to always follow this tungsten-balling procedure in order to TIG weld aluminum.

On the other hand, if you begin TIG welding aluminum using AC current with constant high frequency, the tungsten works just fine! In about five minutes of welding, the pure tungsten will start to form a tiny round ball right on the end of the crayon-shaped tip. And it will do a better job of TIG welding aluminum than when welded with the ritualistic big-balled tungsten! A properly shaped and carefully sharpened tungsten will weld aluminum and magnesium just fine without going through the age-old balling ritual.

CAUTION

Do not touch the tungsten to the aluminum to start the arc! The result of touching the tungsten to the aluminum will be a contaminated tungsten that won't weld anything properly until the aluminum is ground off the tungsten. You will also get a big black spot of soot on your aluminum sample, and soot does not weld.

Anytime you touch the tungsten to the aluminum or the aluminum welding rod to the tungsten while you are welding, you will get a big flash of light from the weld, and you will get a lot of black soot on the weld. You will also get a sizable ball of aluminum on the tungsten. You can't continue to weld when this happens. Stop and clean the ball of aluminum off the tungsten. A sanding belt is a good way to do this, or an 80-grit flap wheel or a bench grinder will also work well. Otherwise, you would have to break the tungsten off at the aluminum ball, and that wastes a lot of expensive tungsten.

WELDING MACHINE SETTINGS

You should begin welding aluminum by practicing on several pieces of scrap before you tackle a job that will fly on an airplane or run on a race car. You should be able to run practice weld beads on small 2x2-inch pieces of thin aluminum sheet material. Practice on 0.020 inch to 0.050-inch thick pieces of scrap aluminum. Next are the standard settings for most AC/DC TIG-welding machines:

- Polarity switch to AC.
- High-frequency switch to Continuous.
- Remote foot pedal switch to Remote.
- Argon gas flowmeter to 20 cfh (cubic feet/hour).
- TIG/Stick switch to TIG.
- Power switch to On.

Note: If you have a square-wave machine, it may or may not have a high-frequency switch.

TIG Welding Tips for Aluminum

- If in doubt about the alloy of the aluminum, use #4043 rod. The 4043 rod works in almost every situation.
- Use the diameter of rod that equals the thickness of metal; i.e., with .065-inch metal, use ^{1}/16-inch rod.
- Use a gas lens cup for aluminum if possible. It makes prettier welds.
- Aluminum butt welding usually "keyholes" the seam. Just keep filling the keyhole with welding rod.
- Have at least three sizes of aluminum welding rod available for all sizes of beads.
- Use only high-quality certified welding rod.
- Don't attempt to weld aluminum after the tungsten has become contaminated.
- Use only pure tungsten for aluminum. Thoriated tungsten contaminates aluminum.

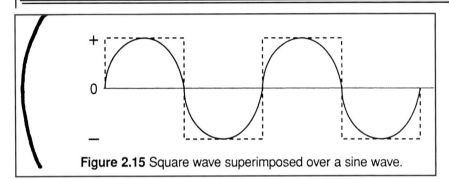

Figure 2.15 Square wave superimposed over a sine wave.

The solid curved line indicates the shape of a normal AC sine wave used in TIG welding. Each peak and valley of the sine wave equals one cycle (hertz). The dash line shows how a square-wave AC welder reshapes the same AC cycle (hertz) to provide longer cleaning time and longer heating time. *Miller Electric Company*

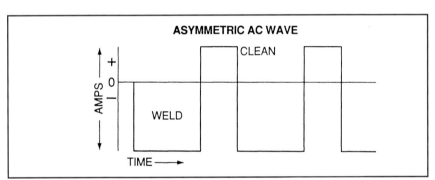

ASYMMETRIC AC WAVE

With an asymmetric AC TIG welder, the clean and weld times can be shaped to better suit the welding process, as illustrated in this drawing provided by Miller Electric. *Miller Electric Company*

CONTROLLING THE ASYMMETRIC POWER SOURCE

Consult this chart by when you are setting up an asymmetric AC TIG welding machine. Especially note the two columns titled "Effect on Bead" and "Effect on Appearance" to decide which adjustment best suits your welding job. As always, practice on scrap pieces first. *Miller Electric Company*

Figure 2.22 The asymmetric power source allows the operator to shape the arc and control the weld bead. Separately or in any combination, the user can adjust current control, frequency (Hz), and balance control to achieve the desired depth of penetration and bead characteristics for each application.

Note: All forms of AC create audible arc noise. Many asymmetric AC combinations, while greatly improving desired weld performance, create noise that may be objectionable to some persons. Hearing protection is always recommended.

The big ceramic cup with the small opening on this TIG torch means that the torch is equipped with a gas lens collet for better welds on aluminum. *Richard Finch*

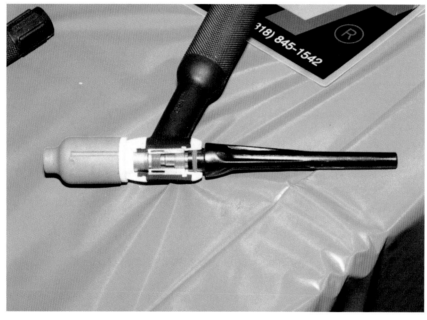

Another gas lens cup TIG torch that is cutaway to show where the water passages are that cool the collet during welding. This is the best kind of torch to use for aluminum welding. *Richard Finch*

STRIKING THE ARC

The easiest way for a TIG-welding beginner to learn to start an arc for welding aluminum is to rest the torch ceramic cup edge on the aluminum surface with the tungsten resting about 1/2 inch from the aluminum. When you depress the foot pedal about halfway, the arc should start, similar to a spark-plug arc starting.

WHY DOES ALUMINUM CONTAMINATE THE TUNGSTEN?

Remember that the temperature of the TIG arc is about 6,000°F and that aluminum melts at about 1,150°F. When the hotter tungsten touches the relatively cooler aluminum puddle, the cooler aluminum wants to flow to the hotter metal by capillary action. It wicks up on the tungsten and temporarily contaminates it. But if you continue to try to TIG weld with aluminum-contaminated tungsten, the 6,000°F heat of the electrode will boil or burn off the aluminum in small amounts that will badly smoke up your weld. So don't try to weld with contaminated tungsten.

ALUMINUM WELD PROCEDURE

Once you have learned to melt a puddle on a piece of aluminum, smoothly dip the end of your welding rod into the puddle, then pull the welding rod back about 1/2 inch. Then continue to dip and pull the welding rod back, and you will see your beautiful weld bead

Here you see two separate trays that hold TIG welding parts. One tray is painted red and it holds 2 percent thoriated tungsten parts for welding steel. The other tray is painted green and it holds pure tungsten for welding aluminum. *Richard Finch*

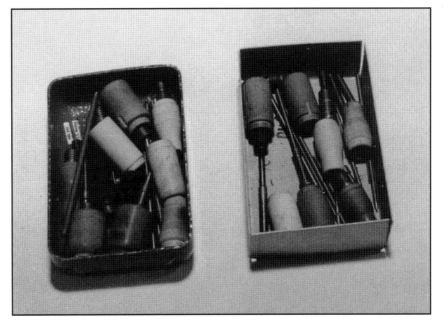

This TIG welder can make the average welder look like a pro. This machine makes it possible to make the special adjustments that are described in the Arc Balance Control chart in this chapter. *Miller Electric Company*

progress. Dip about every two seconds. For practice, say, "dip, dip, dip, dip" and develop a rhythm of dipping the rod into the puddle. A little practice will begin to pay off.

SQUARE-WAVE WELDERS

Welding technology for the twenty-first century includes square-wave technology. In the standard mode, AC welders incorporate a sine wave that is a series of positive and negative pulses of electricity, shaped like half circles, one above the zero current line and one below the zero current line. This cycle of positive and negative pulses occurs 60 times each second, 3,600 times per minute, and 216,000 times per hour. That is how it works in regular AC welding.

But in square-wave welding, the positive and negative pulses stay at their peaks of plus and minus for much longer periods. Rather than the sine wave (rounded corners), the square wave has square corners. This square configuration allows the AC current to spend more time cleaning and more time heating the metal being welded, which is usually aluminum or magnesium.

Square-wave welding is not available in DCSP (direct current, straight polarity) when welding steel. It is only available in AC welding.

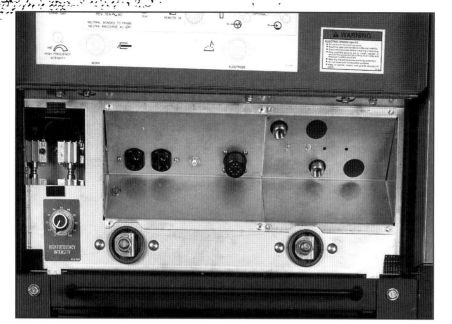

When you lift the hinged door on the front bottom of this machine, you will see the high frequency spark gap copper contacts that must be cleaned and adjusted periodically, usually once a year. *Miller Electric Company*

Flat 0.050-inch thick 6061-T6 aluminum sheet was trimmed and formed into four separate pieces to make this round defroster duct adapter for my airplane. *Richard Finch*

SQUARE-WAVE VARIATIONS

Study the chart in this chapter that illustrates the different settings possible with a full-featured square-wave welding machine. Four major, independently adjustable functions of the asymmetric power source are:

- Frequency in cycles per second (hertz).
- Electrode negative current level in amps.
- Electrode positive current level in amps.
- Balance (the percent of time the electrode is negative).

ADVANTAGES OF SQUARE WAVE

- More efficient control results in higher travel speeds.
- Narrower, more deeply penetrating arc.
- Able to narrow or eliminate the etched zone.
- Improved arc stability.
- Reduced use of high frequency.

LOW-END SQUARE-WAVE WELDERS

The selling price difference between non-adjustable square-wave welders and fully adjustable square-wave welders ranges from $1,300 to $10,000. The low-end square-wave welding machines do a pretty good job on aluminum sheet as thin as 0.010 inch. The top-of-the-line, fully adjustable asymmetric square-wave welding machines can adequately weld a crack in a big aluminum-block V-8 racing engine without preheating, and they can do a beautiful job welding cracks in preheated aluminum-cylinder-head cracks. The choice of machine is determined by the money

Many individual pieces of 6061-T6 aluminum were put together by TIG welding to make this race car oil pan. *Richard Finch*

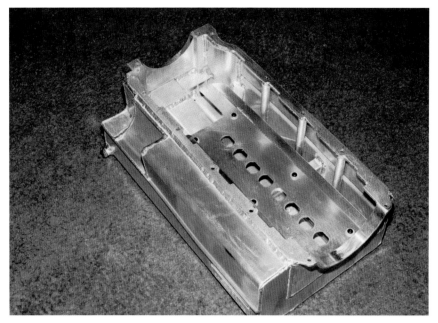

These lightweight aluminum valve covers were welded for this record-holding Bonneville race car. It went 278 miles per hour in 1992. Another local company welded up the sheet aluminum intake manifold. *Richard Finch*

in your budget and the aluminum welding you expect to do.

HIGH FREQUENCY

High-frequency AC current is added to AC or DC current to initiate a spark-jump arc so the tungsten does not have to touch the weld metal to start the arc. It is also added to (superimposed over) the pulsating current of AC welding to make the arc more stable and to keep the arc from going out at lower settings. A lot has been said about the possible negative effects of high-frequency AC welding on televisions and computers in the vicinity. The suggestion is that high frequency can burn out your TV or your computer, and this is a very good possibility.

But you can weld aluminum with AC current and high frequency as close as 20 feet from several active computer systems, and not even make a blip on their screens. All you need is a good ground to carry off any stray high-frequency voltage before it reaches valuable electronic equipment such as computers.

TIG WELDING MAGNESIUM

Magnesium can catch fire and burn, and when it does, just stand back and let it burn. In World War II, the Germans dropped magnesium incendiary bombs on London, and the magnesium fires could not be extinguished. But magnesium does not usually catch fire unless magnesium powder or filings are in the fire.

So don't worry too much about welding magnesium castings. They weld about like aluminum castings, except that magnesium seems to be shinier while it's being TIG welded. During the TIG-welding process, magnesium welds almost exactly like

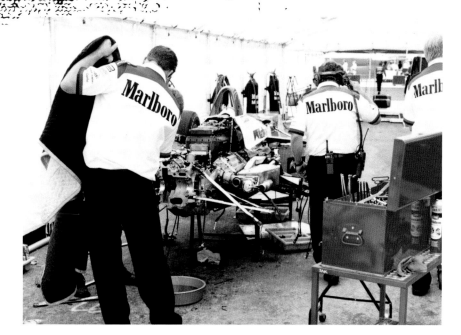

This Indy race car features a lot of TIG welding in the radiator cooling system. Ah, racing! *Richard Finch*

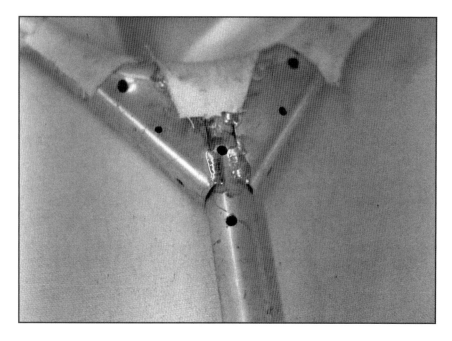

This airplane seat frame is made out of 6061-T6 aluminum and is TIG welded. You see here that 100 percent welds are not always used, just enough weld bead to make the seat strong. *Richard Finch*

aluminum. However, you do want to be sure to use the correct magnesium welding rod. Read Appendix A to find out about magnesium welding rod.

TIG WELDING ALUMINUM HEADS

Typically, aluminum cylinder heads (automotive) and aluminum cylinders (aircraft) are very easy to weld when the need arises to repair cracks, ruined threads, and loose valve seats and valve guides. Like any other aspect of welding, the basic rules apply:

Clean the head or cylinder by completely removing all traces of carbon, preferably by chemical parts cleaning, then rinsing in clear, clean water.

Use a die grinder to V-out the crack or to remove pounded-out metal where the valve seat came loose. In some cases, bits of broken valve seats may still be imbedded in the combustion chamber, so be sure to grind them out.

V-grind all cracks deep enough to ensure 100 percent penetration of the crack when welding, or the unwelded part of the crack will propagate back into the weld.

PREHEAT

You can't easily clamp the head into or onto a steel welding fixture, so you should expect a slight amount

TIG aluminum welding is used to build this radiator and water lines for this Buick V-6 Indy Lights race car cooling system. *Richard Finch*

These aluminum radiators are beautifully welded. *Richard Finch*

of warpage from the welding and heat-treating process. Expect to resurface the head to remove warpage after welding.

Do not expect to preheat an aluminum head by using an oxyacetylene torch. You cannot control the heat of the torch accurately enough to do a proper job of preheating to 350°F. An oven is the only accurate way to preheat a cylinder assembly on a cylinder head. To ensure a complete preheat, the head should be preheated for at least one hour at 350°F immediately before beginning welding.

WELDING ROD

Read Appendix A to find out about the proper rod to use, but 3/32-inch 4043 rod is a good choice to start with. You may also want to have several sticks of 1/16-inch and 5/64-inch rod on hand just in case. Just remember that the diameter of the welding rod has a direct effect on the size of the completed weld bead.

TUNGSTEN AND CUP SIZE

You ought to start with a rather large torch cup, such as a No. 10, and at least a 3/32-inch-diameter pure tungsten, and if that is not enough, use a No. 12 cup and a 1/8-inch pure tungsten.

A water-cooled torch is the best way to weld thick aluminum castings. Air-cooled torches will get too hot and may affect the quality of your welds.

Check out Chapter 2 for information about which welding machines do the best jobs on repair-welding large aluminum castings.

Preparing to install brackets for this aluminum radiator in a 1964 Chevelle street/drag car. *Richard Finch*

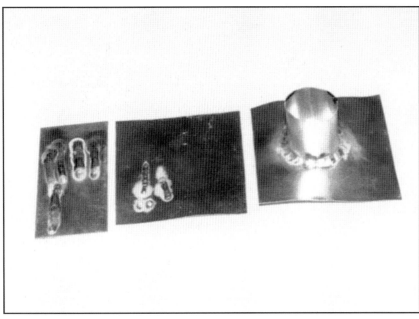

Before you tackle a delicate TIG welding job, practice on some scrap pieces of the same material, as was done here. *Richard Finch*

WELD REPAIR OF VALVE SEATS, ALUMINUM HEADS

One of the facts of life when using aluminum engine cylinder heads is that there are two kinds of aluminum cylinder heads: those that have had valve seats come loose, and those that will have valve seats come loose if run long enough.

Heating and cooling cycles in cast aluminum tend to take out the temper (heat treat) and soften the aluminum. When the aluminum gets soft enough, and the valve has pounded the seat a few million times, the seat often comes loose and really hurts the cylinder and combustion chamber.

But do not fear, loose valve seats in aluminum cylinders and cylinder heads are very easy to repair if you have the proper equipment. Proper equipment includes cleaning and degreasing equipment, preheating equipment, a TIG-welding machine with at least 200 or more amps power (the new square-wave machines are the best), and a milling machine for refinishing the head after it's repair welded.

BUILDUP PROCEDURE

After the head is completely cleaned and preheated, the damaged seat area is welded in nice, smooth layers of weld bead to build up the aluminum high and

TIG welding a larger aluminum tube to the automotive air conditioner evaporator converted it into a very light and efficient engine cooling radiator for a stand-mounted Mazda aircraft engine. Read Chapter 11, "Welding Shop Safety," before TIG welding things that have had oil in them, such as this aluminum evaporator. *Richard Finch*

A converted Mazda rotary engine uses aluminum to make this well-built and intricate oil pan. Preheating this assembly would make it easier to weld. *Richard Finch*

thick enough so there will be plenty of metal to support re-machining the valve pocket out for a new valve seat.

The first time you try valve-seat repair by TIG welding, practice on a scrap cylinder head until you get a good feel for how the bead should look. It's even enjoyable to make TIG weld repairs on aluminum castings. It's a lot like applying clay to build up a clay pot. Proper preparation and welding rod filler material make the job quite easy.

WELD FIXTURE

If the aluminum part you're welding is thin and light, such as a transmission tail-shaft housing, expect it to shrink if you don't clamp it to a steel fixture to hold

it in shape. The steel clamping fixture should be at least 3/8-inch thick, and the aluminum part should be bolted to it before you put it into the oven for preheating.

You should leave the aluminum part bolted to the steel holding fixture while you weld it and until it cools. If you need to heat treat the aluminum part after welding it, the steel holding fixture could be clamped to it. In other words, if you are welding an aluminum tail-shaft housing that weighs 3 pounds, the steel holding plate you bolt it to should weigh at least 15 to 20 pounds. This means that the weight (mass) of the steel holding plate/fixture will be enough to control most of the aluminum casting's tendency to shrink when heated by welding.

Here is quite a nice TIG weld on a radiator expansion tank neck for an engine test stand. Try to make your TIG welds look this nice and smooth. *Richard Finch*

Cut several pieces of scrap 6061-T6 aluminum tubing into angles so you can practice making good welds before you tackle a serious project. *Richard Finch*

The TIG-welded aluminum radiator and aluminum expansion filler tank save several pounds of weight in this race car. *Richard Finch*

Another Indy Lights race car has numerous tanks, pipes, and fittings that are TIG-welded aluminum. Race car and aircraft welders cannot get along without a TIG-welding machine that welds aluminum. *Richard Finch*

Several wing ribs in this right side wing were TIG welded to make sealed-off fuel bays in the wing. Even the space shuttle has a 6061-T6 welded crew compartment for pressure sealing while in orbit. *Richard Finch*

ALL'S WELD THAT ENDS WELL STEEL

MIG WELDING

STEEL and STAINLESS STEEL

High production rates and initial ease of operation make MIG welding very attractive to many aircraft and race car builders. But, not everything is as it seems.

MIG welding is the most difficult of all manual welding processes to master. The reasons why MIG welding is so hard to learn are numerous:

1. The smoke and sparks made by MIG welding make it hard to see the seam to be welded.
2. Once you squeeze the trigger, you are committed to weld at a fixed, unalterable speed.
3. The weld puddle is hard to see because the gun nozzle is in the way.
4. The welder must constantly aim the gun at the weld, meaning that the round tubes and anything but flat surfaces require lots movement by the welder.
5. Choices of electrode wire make lots of difference in weldability and weld quality.
6. Choices of shielding gas contribute to or detract from weldability and weld quality.

How to deal with the problems of MIG welding:

- With better (more-expensive) equipment, you can overcome most of the smoke and sparks, and you will be able to see the weld better.
- Many certified aircraft MIG welders have learned to give short, one- or two-second bursts of weld, thereby manually pulse-welding thin parts to prevent burn-through.
- You will be able to see the MIG weld puddle better if you look at the side of the weld so the gun does not hide your view.
- For welding round tubing, you will need to practice moving your entire body around the tubing for better control of the weld, a solution to number 4 above.
- MIG weld wire metallurgy is improving on a monthly basis. Stay in touch with the major manufacturers of MIG wire to determine the best wire for the jobs you are doing.

It appears that 75/25 gas (75 percent argon and 25 percent CO_2) is the best shielding gas for welding steel, and argon-and-helium for welding aluminum. Stainless-steel MIG welds require 90 percent helium

and 7 percent argon plus CO_2. Again, no set, standard shielding gas is best for every welding situation. You will have to talk to welding gas dealers for the latest information.

FOUR MIG PROCESSES

Four types of welding processes are available with MIG welding. And you say that you thought there was only one kind of MIG welding? There are really four or more uniquely different kinds.

The four basic MIG welding processes are:

- Short-circuit transfer (the most common).
- Globular transfer (used in heavy equipment).
- Spray-arc transfer (for thicker metals, more penetration).
- Pulsed-spray arc transfer (for thinner metals).

SHORT-CIRCUIT TRANSFER

Most of the lower-priced MIG-welding machines use this metal-joining process. In this process, a small-diameter wire is fed through a gun by a variable-speed electric motor, and when the wire touches the grounded base metal, an arc starts and the wire melts off onto the base metal. This process occurs from 60 to 150 times per second, depending on how fast the wire is fed through the gun.

Short-circuit transfer works with a flux-cored wire, a solid wire and shielding gas, and it works with steel, stainless steel, titanium, aluminum, and magnesium, as well as most other weldable metals. The welding arc with short-circuit transfer sounds a lot like bacon frying in a pan.

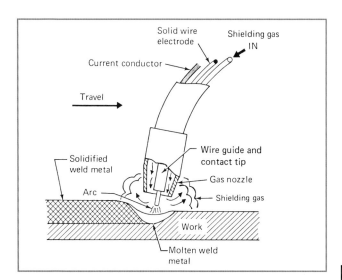

This drawing of a typical MIG-welding process helps illustrate the standard short-circuit arc transfer employed by a MIG-welding machine. *Lincoln Electric Company*

MIG welding two pieces of 1/8-inch steel plate in a T-shape is very easy to do, but this is not very high-quality welding. One tap with a hammer on the backside of the vertical piece and the weld will break. *Richard Finch*

Most MIG welders are easy to set up and operate. This mid-priced machine has a spool of 0.030-inch wire and a drive roll adjustment inside the door. Nothing else needs attention. *Richard Finch*

It's OK to practice MIG welding on straight T-joints, and almost anyone can master this technique in just a few minutes. Practice on tubular parts to learn faster. *Richard Finch*

Here is a typical T-joint welded
with flux-core MIG wire. Flux-core
leaves lots of slag and smoke that
needs to be cleaned off. *Richard Finch*

GLOBULAR TRANSFER

In this MIG-welding process, the welding wire short-circuits at the very start of the weld, but once the arc is established, the heat of the weld arc continues to melt globs of metal off the wire and into the hot weld puddle. The melted-off globs of metal are usually larger in diameter than the electrode wire diameter.

Globular-transfer MIG welding is usually accomplished with the use of straight CO_2 shielding gas only and higher voltages and amps than with short-circuit transfer. Globular-transfer MIG welding also produces more spatter beside the weld than short-circuit-transfer MIG welding, and it is mostly used in fabrication and repair of earth-moving equipment, where welding speed is very important.

SPRAY-ARC TRANSFER

In this MIG-welding process, a stream of tiny metal droplets are "sprayed" off the wire electrode into the weld puddle. These tiny droplets are usually smaller than the diameter of the welding wire. The arc is said to be on all the time once an arc is established.

Spray-arc transfer uses a significantly higher voltage, higher wire-feed speed, and higher amps than short-circuit-transfer MIG welding. As a result, higher metal deposit rates are achieved. Because of the higher heat and higher wire-feed speeds, the weld seam is usually wider, meaning that this process works best in the flat position and for thick metals. Shielding gas mixtures are usually above 90 percent argon, with CO_2 and oxygen added.

The sound made by spray-arc transfer welding is louder and much higher pitched than short-circuit-transfer welding. It has a humming sound.

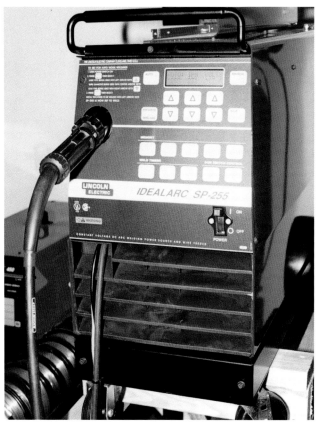

This push-button MIG welder adjusts much like a modern
kitchen microwave oven, with film switches rather than
knobs or dials. *Richard Finch*

This welder has an addéd spot/stitch/seam timer feature that is handy for auto body sheetmetal work, but is not necessary for aircraft and race car welding.
Richard Finch

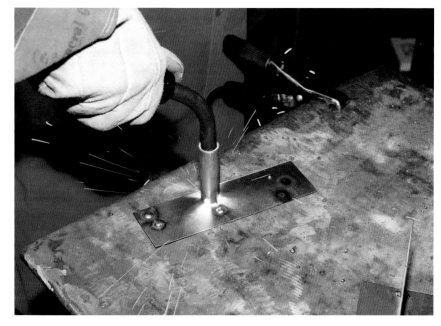

This welder demonstrates the spot timer feature that allows the operator to simply hold the MIG gun with a special four-slot cup against the metal and shoot pre-timed welds.
Richard Finch

PULSED-SPRAY ARC TRANSFER

This could be the best kind of MIG welding for thin-wall tubing when all the characteristics get worked out. A special pulsed-spray arc-transfer welding machine must be used to dial in the special output current, but the same machine will also weld the standard short-circuit MIG welding.

In pulse-spray arc transfer, the special welding machine pulses the welding output to give high current peaks that are set at amp levels that cause the metal transfer to go into a spray. Then the background voltage is set at a level that will maintain the arc between the current peaks.

Because the heat input is lower, pulsed-spray arc transfer allows for welding thinner metals without heat distortion and without burn-through. In most cases, the shielding gas for this process is the same as for spray-arc welding.

WHICH MIG WELDER?

Remember that you are reading this book to become more proficient at performance welding. This means that you are not interested in making 50-percent-OK welds. That means that you want to be able to make aircraft-quality welds in several kinds of metals. These requirements mean that you can't put up with bottom-of-the-line welding equipment.

Flux-core-only MIG welders would then be out of the question. Any time you might save with flux-core MIG welders would be overshadowed by the time it

Sheet-steel seam welds made by a MIG welder are fast and easy to do on flat plate, but trying the seam welds on thin tubing is a whole different skill to learn. *Richard Finch*

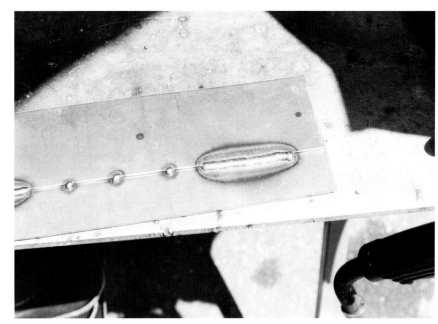

Tim Marr demonstrates the proper two-hand method to accurately control the MIG gun when welding thin-wall tubing on a weld table. *Richard Finch*

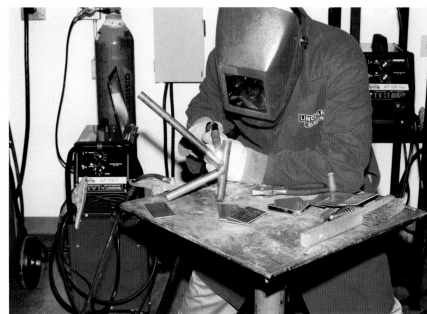

takes you to chip off the flux and file off all the spatter that flux-core welding produces. And then you have to wire brush off the smoke that collects all over the weld.

Another problem with flux-core welding on small-diameter thin-wall tubing is that every time you stop the weld and start again, you should chip off the flux and clean the weld so you won't bury flux when you start the weld again. On one tubular joint, this could be 20 to 30 stops and starts before the weld is completed. Why you might start and stop that many times is explained later in the chapter.

So, let's agree that the bottom-of-the-line flux-core-only welders are best suited to welding tee joints in 1/8-inch plates, and on a flat surface only. No uphill welding, no overhead welding, and for sure, no small round tubes.

HOW MUCH TO SPEND

In order to buy a good-quality, gas-shield MIG welder that will weld all metals including aluminum, expect to spend about $1,800 to $2,500, somewhat more than you would spend for an equivalent TIG-welding machine. The reason for this additional cost is that a machine that will accurately weld thick materials up to 5/16 inch and thin materials down to 0.020 inch tubing is computer-controlled.

CC CV WELDERS

There are several wire-feed welding machines that are just too powerful for delicate aircraft-quality welding. These 300- to 600-amp machines are a must for skyscraper building and bridge welding. Used on the wrong job, they are like to trying to drive a carpet tack

This airplane nose landing gear was factory MIG welded, and the somewhat thick, high weld bead is very evident in this picture. *Richard Finch*

with a 10-pound sledgehammer, you can't do a good job with oversized equipment. You can do a very good job on thin materials with a single-phase 220-volt, 250-amp machine. But, as with most things in welding, try the equipment before you decide on it. The most important factor in MIG welding thin material is the ability of the welder to feed at slow rates, as low as 10 inches of wire per minute and amps of 20 or less. If the machine has a broad range of adjustments up from those settings, that is good.

WIRE SIZE

With most other kinds of welding, the welding rod should be about the same diameter that the weld part is thick. But not so in MIG welding. In MIG welding, the diameter of the welding wire electrode determines the amount of heat required to melt the wire into small drops of metal that make up the weld bead.

The smaller the wire diameter, the less heat it takes to melt the wire. The larger the wire diameter, the more heat it takes to weld and melt the wire. For 0.035-inch wall thickness tubing, you need 0.023-inch-diameter steel welding wire. If you are welding together 0.750-inch-thick steel plates, then 0.050-inch welding wire works better. Wire diameter is another variable in MIG welding. It's a good idea to experiment with small, 5-pound spools of welding wire until you determine which size is best for your purpose.

WIRE ALLOY

To improve starting characteristics and weld penetration characteristics, there are more than 30 different MIG-welding wire alloys. It is safe to presume, then,

Aircraft-quality MIG welding is easy to spot in this Kitfox steel-tube fuselage longeron and cluster weld.
Richard Finch

Another cluster weld on a Kitfox steel-tube airplane fuselage shows the thicker-than-usual weld bead that clearly indicates MIG welding.
Richard Finch

that soon there should be some metallurgical break-throughs in determining the best wire electrode for welding 4130 chrome-moly steel and stainless steel.

STARTING TO MIG WELD

It is really easy to load a spool of welding wire into most MIG-welding machines. Just make sure that the free end of the wire is snipped off square and that there are no kinks to hang up when the wire is feeding through the hose, liner, and through the MIG gun. Once the wire is passed through the drive rolls and into the liner, the trigger on the gun will feed the wire on through.

Once the wire is fed through the gun, back off the roller-tension adjustment so there is no drag at all when the wire is manually pulled out of the nozzle.

Then clip off the excess wire and make the proper tension adjustment.

To adjust for proper wire tension, put the nozzle against a rigid non-conductive surface, such as the cement floor of the shop. Next, squeeze the gun trigger with the machine turned on, and while holding the gun against the floor, begin to adjust the roller tension tighter until you feel the wire pushing the gun nozzle away from the floor. At that exact point, the tension is properly adjusted. Too loose and the wire will not feed; too tight and the rollers will wear out prematurely.

AIRCRAFT SEAT WELDING

During the eight-year production run of Aerostar six-passenger aircraft at the Santa Maria, California,

MIG welding is ideal for adding small, thin metal tabs to aircraft and race car tubular framework because very little heat is needed to spot-weld small pieces. Oxyacetylene would require much more heat to fuse the tab to the tubular part. *Richard Finch*

This tack weld was obviously made with flux-core MIG wire. The slag needs to be chipped off before welding more. *Richard Finch*

airplane factory, over 800 of the twin-engine executive airplanes were built, certified, and sold. Each airplane had six seats that were made by welding up 3/4-inch square 4130 steel tubing into seat frames. More than 4,800 steel frame seats were welded together during that eight year period.

At first, the seats were TIG (Heliarc) welded, but after building about 1,000 seats, with each seat taking six to eight hours apiece to weld together, it was decided to MIG weld the seats to increase production.

A couple of certified TIG welders volunteered to take the aircraft welding certification test by MIG welding the coupons. They passed the test easily, and so began building seats out of 0.032 inch wall 3/4-inch square tubing. The first six seats built by MIG welding were tested to destruction by loading them in all

directions from 9 Gs to as much as 27 Gs. None of the six seats failed any part of the test. It took considerably more loading to bend but not break the seats.

So MIG welding production on the seats began and it was soon found that they could build four to six times as many seats in a given period as they could when they were TIG welding them. The conversion to the MIG process was a complete success. MIG welding was much faster, and it can be equally effective in other aircraft welding production situations.

STRESS RELIEVING

An important aspect of building more than 4,800 steel-frame seats, both by TIG and MIG welding, is that they did not post-heat stress-relieve a single seat. And not one of the seats ever developed stress

Compare this tack weld to the one in the previous photo. This one was made with MIG and a 75/25 mix of gas shielding, leaving much less slag and smoke. *Richard Finch*

This practice MIG weld was made with flux-core wire, as evidenced by the excessive flux and smoke. *Richard Finch*

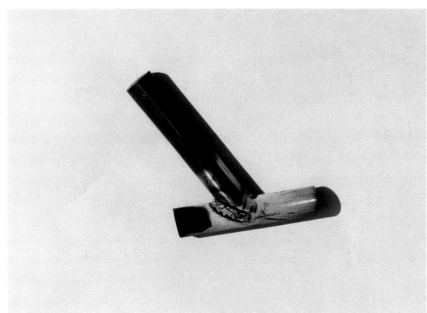

cracks. The age-old habit of oxyacetylene heating all the MIG and TIG welds to cherry or blood red after welding to supposedly stress-relieve the welds was not considered. Obviously, from the 100 percent lack of post-welding cracks, reheating the seat frames wasn't needed.

Conversely, if the post-weld reheating process had been tried, it would have likely induced stress and caused cracks. Read Chapter 5 for additional information about stress relieving after welding and the reasons you can't properly do it with an oxyacetylene torch.

MIG WELDING TIPS

- If at all possible, always weld in the flat position for better quality welds. This means not vertical, not horizontal, and for sure, not overhead.
- Never weld the "real" part until you have tested all the machine settings, amps, wire speed in fpm, gas flow, and especially weld accessibility.
- Always run a couple of test coupons on scrap material to make sure the machine settings and the operator are ready. Notice that the welder (operator) is a big factor.
- Always use anti-spatter spray or dip jelly to prevent spatter buildup in the gun nozzle.
- Be sure to protect painted surfaces from smoke and spatter from the weld.
- Never MIG weld where pets or people can watch the arc. Ultraviolet light is emitted from the arc, and ultraviolet rays can cause eye cataracts and skin cancer over time. On a short-term basis,

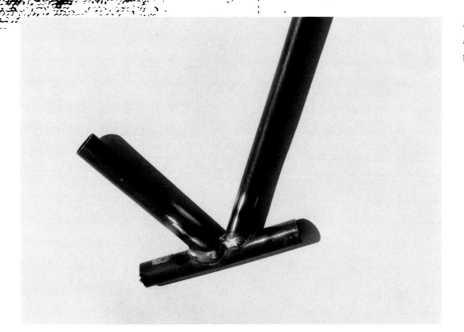

A typical practice weld using 75/25 argon/CO_2 gas leaves a large bead but no smoke or spatter. *Richard Finch*

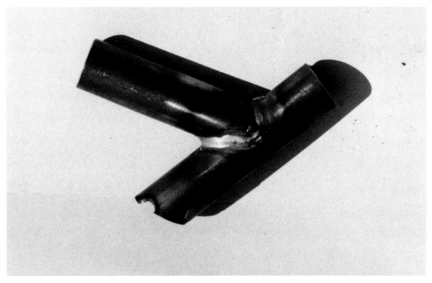

Practice your MIG welds on scrap pieces of tubing before starting your serious projects. The practice weld shown here is average and acceptable. *Richard Finch*

welding eye flash is painful. It causes late-night eye itching.

- When MIG welding stainless-steel sheet, be sure to back up the weld seam with copper strips or welder's ceramic-fiber paste to prevent atmospheric contamination in the weld.
- When MIG welding stainless-steel sheet tubing, always back-gas purge the inside of the tubing to prevent weld contamination.
- Be your own automatic "stitch timer" when welding thin metal, such as 0.020-inch to 0.050-inch thickness. Squeeze the trigger, weld a couple of seconds until you see a melt-through starting, then let up and let the weld cool and solidify for a couple of seconds, then squeeze the trigger and weld a couple of seconds more. Some of the biggest and best manufacturing companies weld tubular structures this way, with great results.

Practice this procedure and you will soon develop the proper rhythm.

- Remember that dirt does not weld. Clean your parts properly before welding.
- Always keep the MIG gun cable from being twisted and tangled. Never stand on the cable while you are welding. The reason is that the wire inside the cable will not feed smoothly if the cable is twisted or if you stand on the cable.
- Change the cups and the copper collets often, because dirty cups and worn collets reduce the quality of the weld.
- Never watch the weld from behind the MIG gun because you can't see the puddle that way.
- Always watch the weld from the side of the MIG gun, where you will be able to see the wire melt off in the puddle.
- And most important of all, never be embarrassed if

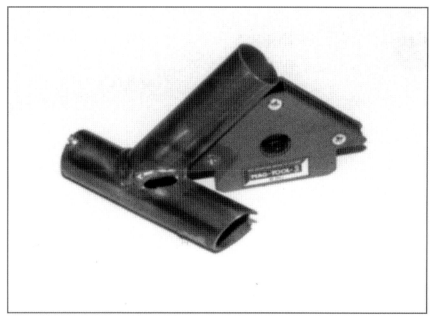

Another practice weld on 7/8-inch x 0.035-inch wall tubing shows what can happen if you don't watch closely enough. This hole in the weld should be cut out, patched, and gas-welded to repair. *Richard Finch*

Two basic controls adjust most MIG-welding machines. On this welder, the bottom knob adjusts wire-feed rate. You should adjust the amps knob by sound for good heat and penetration and the wire feed speed for the smoothest arc. *Richard Finch*

you have to cut out a bad MIG weld because it isn't sound. With a proper air-operated cut-off tool, it's not much trouble to cut out a bad weld on tubing. Then just re-do it properly.

MIG WELDING STAINLESS STEEL

The same polarity setting that you used for welding steel is also used for welding stainless steel. That polarity is DCEP (DC electrode positive). The MIG gun is positive and the work is negative. The only time to change polarity when MIG welding is when you change from gas-protected to flux-core wire.

A noticeable effect of MIG welding stainless steel is that there will be considerable heat staining of the metal in the weld heat-affected zone. But there is a solution to the darkening of the stainless steel. Several companies make an acid-based cleaner that works very well. Use rubber gloves, of course, and with a cloth, wipe the weld down with the cleaner, then neutralize it with another cloth soaked in clear water. It comes clean like magic.

BACKSIDE PROTECTION

Stainless steel is very prone to crystallizing if it's exposed to air at welding temperature. Old welders call it sugar in the weld, meaning that the metal has crystallized, and when this happens, the weld will crack sooner or later. The weld on the top side (front side) will look OK, but the backside looks like a tiny field of volcanic rocks. It's OK to make this happen on scrap pieces of stainless steel just to see how it looks and to break-test the weld to see just how weak it can be. But don't let this happen to good stainless-steel parts. There are several ways to

The proper stance for starting a MIG weld. Note that the operator's helmet is up while the gun is aimed, his left hand helps guide the gun, and his right hand is ready to squeeze the trigger. *Richard Finch*

The next step in starting a MIG weld is to nod your head, causing the helmet to fall in place. If you have an electronic-lens helmet, you can aim the MIG gun with the helmet down and you're ready to weld. *Richard Finch*

Three tack welds made with a MIG welder hold the three tubes in place. Try this cluster assembly several times before you attempt to weld a serious project on an airplane fuselage. *Richard Finch*

Practice, practice, practice. Scrap
tubing as shown here can be
purchased from several different
tubing supply houses. *Richard Finch*

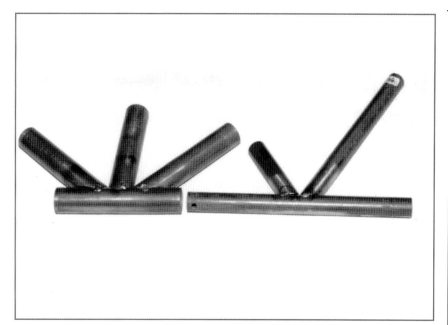

MIG welding a steel radiator brace
for an aluminum radiator in a 1964
drag/street car. *Richard Finch*

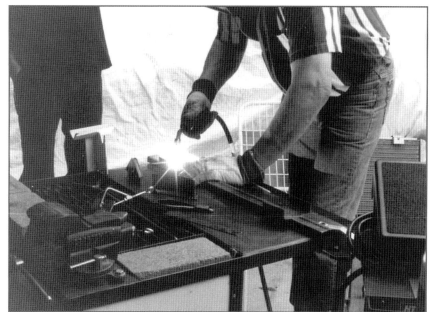

Before welding anything serious,
run a practice bead like this one to
make sure the amps and wire feed
speed are set correctly.
Richard Finch

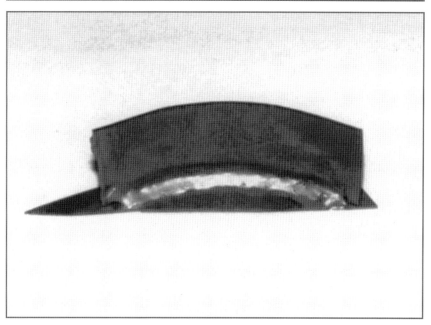

This rolling chassis for a circle-track race car was MIG welded to speed up the fabrication time. *Richard Finch*

This race car is actually a two-thirds-scale Baby Grand Stocker powered by a four-cylinder motorcycle engine. The rolling chassis is MIG-welded mild-steel tubing. *Baby Grand Manufacturing Company*

A new Baby Grand race car sits on a roll-around assembly table, waiting for final assembly. *Baby Grand Manufacturing Company*

This is an excellent example of why MIG welding is the choice for many race car fabricators. The side-impact frame tubing has lots of inches of MIG-weld seams. *Baby Grand Manufacturing Company*

Bare, powder-coated, MIG-welded race car frames sit on fabricated steel roll-around stands, waiting for final assembly. *Baby Grand Manufacturing Company*

protect the backside of stainless-steel welds from atmospheric contamination.

BACK-GASSING

Say these two words to a certified aircraft welder or nuclear power welder, and they will instantly know what you're talking about. You already know that you must have shielding gas on the welded side of your MIG welds to protect the metal from atmospheric (or air-oxygen and nitrogen) contamination. But the backside of the weld is also being heated to above the melting temperature, so it must be protected to a level equal to the gas protection you've provided for the weld puddle.

Any inert gas works well for back-gas protection of stainless-steel welds, but argon is the most common inert gas, so it's best to use this for back-gas purging. In a tubular assembly such as a stainless-steel exhaust-header assembly, simply close off all the openings with masking tape, put an argon hose in one end of the manifold, and punch a pencil-sized hole in the other end of the manifold so the argon will flow through the pipe. Then purge for 5 to 10 minutes at 10 cfh.

To purge a flat seam, a copper heat-sink plate with a half-round groove to flow argon through works very well. But in quick, one-time situations, a simple cardboard V can be taped to the backside of the seam to provide an argon backing path for welding. Always make sure the argon flows all the way through the back up dam and out the other end. Use flow rates of 5 to 10 cfh to back-gas purge.

MIG WELDING TITANIUM

The data books give MIG wire numbers for titanium welding, but since titanium is so prone to hydrogen contamination while it's being welded, the best way to fusion-weld titanium is with the TIG process in a vacuum chamber. MIG welding titanium is possible, but it's an experimental process, and welds should be tested before use.

Dye-penetrant inspection testing is one way to test without damage to the metal assembly. Ultrasonic testing is another non-destructive testing method, and X-ray inspection is a third possibility.

WELD THAT WELL

CHAPTER 8

MIG WELDING
ALUMINIUM
MAGNESIUM

MIG welding is completely adequate and very fast when welding truck toolboxes, diesel fuel tanks, brackets for trucks and tractors, and any other welding job where the aluminum is 1/8-inch thick or thicker. As a matter of welding history, some writers claim that MIG welding was first invented to weld aluminum cleaner and faster than TIG or stick welding.

Although aluminum MIG welding is the real solution for welding truck bodies and other commercial equipment, it is not generally used for thinner aluminum, such as aircraft nose cowlings, fuel tanks, radiators, and other applications where the aluminum to be welded is less than 0.040 inch thick. TIG is the preferred method for thinner aluminum.

WELDABLE ALUMINUM

Beginning with the strongest weldable aluminum, 6061 has the highest tensile strength at 45,000 psi in the T6 heat-treated condition. Next comes 5052 at 41,000 psi in the heat-treated condition, but only 29,000 psi in the non-heat-treated condition. Lowest on the strength scale for weldable aluminum is 1100, almost pure aluminum, at only 13,000 psi tensile strength.

Alloy 5052 aluminum is often used to make airplane fuel tanks and race car water-expansion tanks because it forms better with less tendency to crack than 6061 aluminum. Although 1100 alloy aluminum is very easy to form and weld, it is seldom used in aircraft or race car construction because it's too weak and it dents very easily.

A notable use of weldable 6061-T6 aluminum is in the crew compartment of the four U.S. space shuttles. In order to pressurize a compound-curved structure the size of the space shuttle, welded seams in 6061-T6 aluminum were selected as the best way to achieve a strong, leakproof structure. Therefore, 6061 aluminum is a good choice for weldable airplane and race car components.

NON-WELDABLE ALUMINUM

Of the popular aluminum alloys, the two strongest are not weldable. These alloys are 2024 and 7075. While you can run a so-so weld bead on either of these alloys, a significant crack usually follows the molten puddle to the extent that you can actually watch the metal crack within seconds of being welded, as the weld area cools. Aluminum alloy 2024 makes strong formed-and-riveted or bolted structures. Alloy 7075 makes good high-strength fittings, but

don't try to weld them. The tensile strength of 2024-T4 is 68,000 psi. The tensile strength of 7075-T6 is 82,000 psi. A good rule to follow is that if a machined aluminum fitting has not been welded at the time of manufacture, it is probably non-weldable.

HEAT TREATING ALUMINUM

It's often beneficial to heat treat 5052 or 6061 aluminum parts after fabrication by forming and welding. There are two methods for heat treating aluminum: *solution heat treating* and *precipitation heat treating.*

Solution heat treating is done by dipping the aluminum part into a bath of very hot brine solution and holding the part there for several minutes, depending on its mass (weight). After this dip, the part is immediately removed from the brine and dipped in cold water. The temperature of the brine tank is usually 900° to 1,000°F, and the cold water tank is usually below 50°F.

Precipitation heat treating is done by placing the aluminum part in a very hot oven, heat soaking the part for a specified time, and then curing the part in 70° to 90°F still air for another specified time period, usually 18 to 24 hours.

Heat treating aluminum cannot be properly done with an oxyacetylene torch because of the specific requirement for a very thorough and long period of accurate heating. Consult the following chart to see what it takes to heat treat an average-sized airplane rib or bracket weighing less than 5 pounds.

If it becomes necessary to weld an aluminum part that was originally heat treated, it should be heat treated again after welding to regain its strength. For instance, if you make a weld repair on a 6061-T6 part, with a tensile strength of 45,000 psi, welding it reduces its strength to as low as 18,000 psi in the weld zone. It then slowly regains part of its strength within 24 hours after welding. The as-welded strength will be between 18,000 and 35,000 psi.

One sure way to determine the as-welded strength is to do a Brinell ball-indent test on the weld area. The deeper the small ball deforms the aluminum, the softer it is. Brinell hardness testers are light and portable, and every welding fabrication shop that does aluminum welding repairs should have one. Several Brinell testers are about the size of a big pair of Vise-Grip pliers and operate in a similar manner by pinching the sheet metal between the jaws of the tester.

ALUMINUM MIG WELDING NOTES

Aluminum welding wire is much less stiff than steel or stainless-steel MIG wire, and it kinks and tangles very easily. For this reason, it does not push through the average 10-foot-long MIG gun cable very well. There are two solutions to this common problem:

Remove the wound-steel-core liners from your standard MIG gun cable and replace them with Teflon-lined cable liners that reduce friction inside the cable. Most MIG-gun and MIG-welding-machine manufacturers can supply special Teflon lines for their cables.

Buy a spool gun type of MIG welding gun. Spool guns have a drive motor mounted right on the gun, so the aluminum wire will only be pushed 6 to 8 inches rather than 10 feet as with standard MIG welders. One well-known brand of spool guns is Cobramatic. Spool guns can only utilize small 2 1/2- to 4-pound rolls of aluminum wire, because a full-sized roll of wire would be too cumbersome on the gun.

If you plan to do a lot of aluminum MIG welding, consider trying either a Teflon liner for your standard gun or a spool-gun attachment.

Solution Heat Treat Temps for Aluminum

Alloy	Temp °F	Quench	Temper
2017	950	Cold water	T4
2117	950	Cold water	T4
2024	950	Cold water	T4
6061	980	Cold water	T4
7075	875	Cold water	T4

Precipitation Heat Treat Temps for Aluminum

Alloy	Temp °F	Aging Time	Temper
2024	æ	æ	æ
6061	325	18 hours	T6
7075	250	24 hours	T6

Aluminum MIG welding works very well on thicker sections like this 1/8-inch plate welded to 1/8-inch wall tubing. A special MIG gun called a Cobramatic is used to ensure smooth wire feed right at the nozzle. *Richard Finch*

There are two U-shaped terminal tabs at the top of this 120-volt MIG-welding machine. When the machine is used for flux-core-wire welding, the tabs are positioned fore and aft as can be seen here. When aluminum welding with gas shielding, turn the tabs to 90 degrees, one above and one below. This machine is not an AC welder as in TIG welding.
Richard Finch

ALUMINUM COUPONS

One of the largest truck-body manufacturers in the world uses MIG welding extensively in making permanent, waterproof seams in the 0.050-inch-thick aluminum skins of their trailers. Their chief engineer specifies that no welds will be done without first running a set number of weld samples, called coupons.

The reason for doing this extra work is that aluminum MIG welds can look good and appear fully integrated or penetrated into the base metal, when, in fact, the weld is just laying on top of the metal. The solution for this lack of fusion, of course, is to turn up the heat on the welder. The reason for not just turning up the heat as a matter of practice is that too much heat will burn (melt) holes in the aluminum, and holes in aluminum are very time consuming to repair.

In factories, coupons can be tested in special pull-test machines. In small workshops, a suitable, but less scientific, testing method can be utilized. We call it the bench-vise-and-hammer test. Just weld up your samples and put one end in your bench vise. Then, with a hammer, hit the sample on the other end, on the backside of the weld. If the sample can be bent 90 degrees toward the weld by hitting it with a hammer, and not crack or break, your weld is pretty good. If it breaks or even starts to crack on the backside of the weld, you didn't get sufficient penetration, because you should have used more heat. So turn up the heat on the welding machine and make more test pieces. For aluminum MIG welding, a good-size coupon would be a 3x3-inch square, making a 3x6-inch coupon when it's butt- or seam-welded together.

This same coupon test process works for all other types of welding, too. Until you become very familiar with the performance of your specific welding equipment, you should test your TIG and gas welds this same way.

MIG welding a steel bracket in place for the aluminum radiator in a 1964 Chevelle. The MIG machine is a 220-volt, gas-shield model that will also weld aluminum. *Richard Finch*

ALUMINUM POLARITY

As you remember from Chapter 6, aluminum must be either TIG welded using AC current and continuous high frequency for cleaning or TIG welded with AC current utilizing square-wave technology.

But when you MIG weld aluminum, you don't use AC current. You use DC current, straight polarity, and you still use argon shielding gas. And because of the fact that aluminum oxidizes so fast, you can expect to have to flow more argon than usual to protect the weld from contamination. Rather than adjusting your flowmeter for 20-cfh argon flow as when you weld steel, you may need to adjust for 30 to 50 cfh when you MIG weld aluminum.

ALUMINUM SPATTER

When you're MIG welding aluminum, you'll notice that the gun nozzle picks up a lot more spatter than it does when you're MIG welding steel. Be sure to dip or spray the nozzle often when you're welding aluminum. After

Suggested Welding Alloys for Aluminum and Magnesium

Aluminum Alloy	Electrode	AWC Spec.
1100	ER1100 or ER4043	A5.10
3003,3004	ER1100 or ER5356	
5052,5454	ER5556 or ER5356	
6061-6063	ER4043	

Magnesium Alloy	Electrode	AWC Spec.
AZ10A	ERAZ61A	A5.19
AZ31B	ERAZ61A	
AZ80A	ERAZ92A	
ZE10A	ERAZ61A	
ZE21A	ERAZ61A	
AZ92A	ERAZ92A	
HK31A	ERAZ33A	

Note: Read Chapter (insert number) for more detailed reasons to use a specific welding wire for MIG welding aluminum or magnesium.

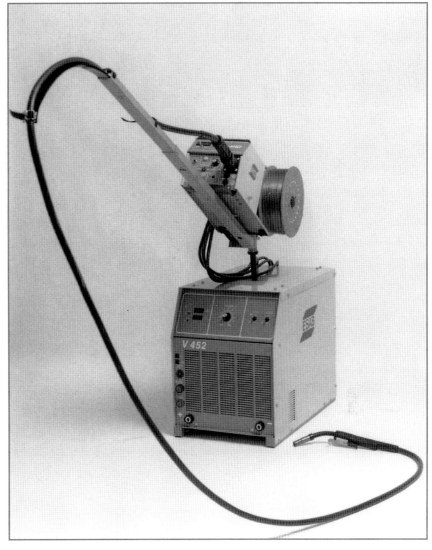

This large, heavy-duty 400-volt commercial MIG-welding machine features a separate wire-feed module. *ESAB Welding & Cutting Products*

the first 30 minutes of welding, take the gun nozzle off and scrape the spatter out of the inside. If you neglected to coat the nozzle with spray or jelly, the spatter may stick permanently to the nozzle, making it necessary to replace it with a new one. If you let spatter coat the inside of the nozzle, the argon gas cannot flow properly, and your aluminum welds will start to turn black and sooty because of the lack of shielding gas protection.

CLEANING ALUMINUM

Do not try to weld dirty, oily, or paint-covered aluminum. It must be very clean to weld properly. At the very least, remove all grease and oil with acetone shortly before welding. You will also notice that aluminum oxidizes in the heat-affected zone even while you're welding. To remove this instant oxidation, keep a small stainless-steel wire brush

handy and wire brush the weld-seam area just before you start welding.

BACK-GASSING

It is not necessary to back-gas purge thin aluminum while welding as is required when welding stainless steel, but using copper backup strips on the backside of the weld seam will prevent burn-through in most cases.

MIG WELDING MAGNESIUM

Welding magnesium and aluminum are similar procedures. Extra care should be taken to weld magnesium in an area that is free of flammable materials in case the magnesium catches fire. As you will read in Chapter 12 on welding safety, if magnesium catches fire, you cannot extinguish the fire with water or any type of fire extinguisher.

CHAPTER
9

GAS WELDING STEEL and STAINLESS STEEL

Gas welding (OFW, oxy-fuel welding) is the basis for learning other, more modern kinds of welding, such as TIG and MIG. Learning to properly control the 6,300°F heat of the flame to fusion-weld 4130 chrome-moly steel, which melts at 2,785°F and vaporizes at 5,500°F, is an art, much like playing a musical instrument. And like mastering a musical instrument, mastering gas welding can be very satisfying.

BEWARE OF OBSOLETE INFORMATION

Textbooks that claim to be the newest printing on the subject of gas welding have been known to contain reprints of articles written in 1935, 1940, 1953, and 1963. Everything has changed since those years, metallurgically speaking. Reflecting these changes, this chapter contains the most recent, state-of-the-art information about welding filler metals available at the beginning of the twenty-first century.

SAME BASIC PROCESS

For the past 75 to 80 years, the physics of mixing equal parts of compressed oxygen and acetylene gas at 1 to 15 psi has produced flame temperatures of 6,300°F, measured at the inner flame cone. The chemistry of the gases has not changed, and the process of consuming the two gases in a fire is still the same as it was in 1910 and 1920. The only factor that's changed is smaller, more accurate burning wands, or torches, as they're called today. Each manufacturer strives to make smoother operating and more dependable gas welding equipment so their products will sell better than their competitors'.

In this chapter, several pictures of early gas-welding equipment have been provided to let you see its slow evolution. Compare the old stuff to what is available today. The biggest change has been the much smaller gas bottles around now. Old bottles weighed over 300 pounds, and current portable bottles weigh 25 to 30 pounds.

STARTING RIGHT

Several years ago, a friend asked me to help him gas weld an engine mount for his plywood-construction experimental airplane. As I pulled my car up in front of his garage, I saw him welding, with big pops of gas explosions and sparks flying 10 feet or more in all directions. Remember he was building a plywood airplane, so there was sawdust and wood scraps all over the floor, and the sparks were landing in all this flammable material!

Thankfully, his workshop, his airplane, and his house didn't catch fire and burn! His welding problem was that his acetylene regulator was adjusted for 12 psi (15 psi is red-line), and his oxygen regulator was set at 25 psi. His excessively high gas pressures, combined with a very dirty welding torch tip, were conspiring to oxidize all his welds.

Once I cut his oxygen and acetylene pressures down to 4 psi and cleaned his welding tip, he was able to work really pretty weld beads with no popping and almost no sparks coming off his welds. Within 10 or 15 minutes, he had gone from a bad welder to a rather good welder. And I convinced him to sweep the floor and have a water hose handy to extinguish fires, just in case.

GAS PRESSURES

If your gas welding torch is in good condition (if it isn't, by all means, fix it), you should always weld with 4 to 6 psi gas pressures, both oxygen and acetylene. You'll use much higher oxygen pressures when cutting through 3- or 4-inch-thick steel plate, because the cutting process is called an oxidizing cut. You can even cut thick steel plate with oxygen only once the oxidizing cut has been started by oxygen plus acetylene. Just remember, too much oxygen pressure will oxidize your weld. Stick with low pressure for fusion welding steel.

CLEAN YOUR TIPS

You should never begin a day or an hour of gas welding until you have thoroughly cleaned your gas torch welding tips. Every time you weld, tiny, and sometimes large, sparks fly up from the molten weld puddle. These sparks are really red-hot pieces of metal, and they stick to every piece of metal they touch, including the inside and outside of your copper welding tips.

To clean your tip, first ream out the inside of the tip with the largest wire reamer that will easily fit inside the tip. Next, scrape the outside of the tip to remove all carbon and slag that are sticking to the tip. Then, carefully file the opening area of the tip to remove the slag that is still sticking to the end of the tip. Finally, wipe the outside of the tip with the acetone cloth that you use to clean the welding rod. If you have shop air, you can blow out the inside of the tip as well.

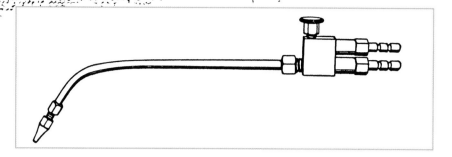

Oxyacetylene welding torches like this one were the only way to weld in the early 1920s. *Richard Finch Collection*

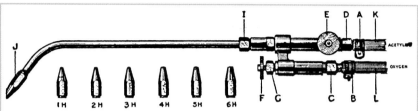

Figure 246.—Equal Pressure Welding Blowpipe. *A*, Clamp for Holding Acetylene Hose on Nipple; *B*, Clamp for Holding Oxygen Hose on Nipple; *C*, Union Nut on Oxygen Hose Nipple; *D*, Union Nut on Acetylene Hose Nipple; *E*, Needle Valve for Controlling Acetylene Supply; *F*, Needle Valve for Controlling Oxygen Supply; *G*, Stuffing Nut on Oxygen Needle Valve; *I*, Union Nut for Disengaging or Changing Angle of Barrel of Blowpipe; *J*, Interchangeable Welding Tip, Size *7H*, *1H*, *2H*, *3H*, *4H*, *5H*, and *6H* are Extra Interchangeable Welding Tips.

A more complex oxyacetylene torch set from 1925 featured the same parts that are still in use in the twenty-first century. This one just looks old. *Richard Finch Collection*

The reason you should always start by cleaning the welding torch tip is that all the slag that sticks to the tip acts like a heat collector and causes the tip to heat up more than usual. It's this overheating that causes the torch to pop.

CAUSES OF POPPING

Oxyacetylene torches pop because they are overheated. They become overheated for several reasons:

1. When you're using a tip that's too small for the work you're welding, you keep putting the torch closer to the metal in order to make a good puddle, and then the heat from the weld reflects back to the torch body, causing it to overheat. When the torch tip overheats, the gases inside the tip will explode, causing welding sparks to fly all over the place. This is a dangerous situation. To solve this problem, change to the next size larger tip. Sometimes you have to go two or three sizes larger to stop this overheat popping.

2. Another reason for occasional popping of the torch is just a dirty tip. Look at the tip, and if slag is stuck to the tip's last 2 or 3 inches, stop welding and clean the tip.
   The reason that dirty tips tend to pop is that the dirt/slag on the tip collects heat a lot faster than

a clean, new tip does. It actually helps to sand the tip to its natural copper color to reduce popping. Some welders spray MIG welding anti-spatter on their gas welding tips to reduce spatter buildup, and that solution works well also.

3. If you are welding into a corner, the flame and heat will be reflected back toward the tip. Again, overheated tips contribute to torch popping. If this is the cause of popping, change the torch angle to make it reflect less heat back on you and the tip. If an overheated tip is causing popping, the problem will go away.

4. If your welding tip is badly worn, it will not produce a symmetrical flame. A crooked or badly shaped flame will not produce the proper heat, and the torch will always pop, no matter what you do. If your favorite torch tip has been used for more than five years, it's probably worn out. Buy a new tip and see if your welding improves.

NEUTRAL FLAME

One thing that is consistent with most welding textbooks is that they usually show drawings of three different oxyacetylene welding flames. The three flames are oxidizing (too much oxygen), carburizing (too much acetylene and soot), and neutral (equal pressures and equal amounts of both gases). You should know by now that no welding job requires an oxidizing flame or a carburizing flame. A neutral flame is the only flame for gas welding.

Adjusting for a neutral flame is easy. You start by turning the acetylene valve on the torch to about one-third to one-half turn open and light the torch with a flint striker (not a butane lighter!). As soon as the acetylene flame lights, quickly open the oxygen valve to about one-third turn. At this point, you will have an almost-neutral flame, but continue to adjust the oxygen and acetylene valves until the inner flame core becomes a single flame.

THREE FLAME SOUNDS

With one particular size welding tip, you can adjust the flame for three different heat ranges, judged by three different sounds. The three sounds are: a soft whisper, a medium hiss, and a noisy hiss. While the inner-cone temperature of all three flames is still 6,300°F, the volume of heat (BTUs) is different for each flame.

It works better to braze and weld very thin material with a soft flame. A medium flame works well for fusion welding materials such as exhaust-pipe tubing and 4130 chrome-moly structures. The noisy, hissing flame is a partial solution when welding thicker materials such as angle brackets, usually from mild steel. At no time should you try to weld important safety-critical parts with a loud, hissing flame, because the actual flame pressure tends to boil and misshape the metal. Just change to a welding tip one or two sizes larger to eliminate the need for a really loud flame.

GAS WELDING SPARKS

There will always be a few intermittent sparks that come out of the weld puddle when you are properly gas welding steel. These sparks are tiny, and they seldom travel more than 12 inches before they die out.

If you are getting a constant shower of sparks with some that fly 5 to 10 feet away from your weld puddle, stop welding and fix this obvious problem. This many sparks indicate that you are burning and boiling the metal. You are making weak, crystallized welds. Quite likely, you need one size larger tip and a softer flame. It may be that you even need two sizes larger tip. Try it and see which works best.

If the part is important, you should inspect the weld closely and consider cutting out the bad weld bead with an air cut-off wheel. Then start over and do the weld right. One big difference in gas welding today, compared to 25 to 50 years ago, is the advent of air tools. Welds that can be cut out in 30 seconds with an air cut-off wheel would have taken 15 minutes to saw and file out in 1940.

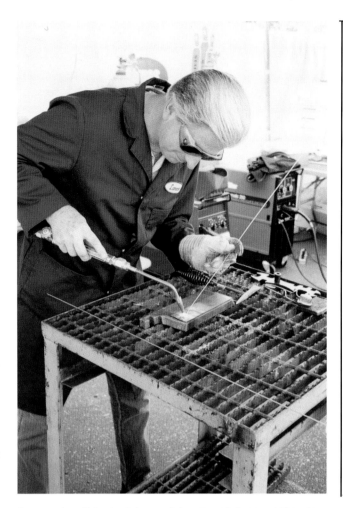

An example of typical heavy-duty oxyacetylene welding is this application of hard-facing metal to a 3/4-inch-thick steel plate. Regardless of the high-tech or low-tech aspects of a weld fabrication shop, *every* weld shop should have an oxyacetylene welding setup. *Richard Finch*

GAS WELDING TUBULAR FRAMES

Take a close look at the photos in this chapter and copy the particleboard welding table for large framework projects. A picture can be equal to a thousand words of written instruction. This type of low-production frame assembly is a time-proven process, and it works very well. Copy it, and your project will be a success.

LEARN BY LOOKING

This chapter includes several photos of imperfect, but acceptable, aircraft-quality welds. Go out to the shop and set up some practice welds to get the feel of how the sample welds were done. After you have completed a few welds, inspect them and compare them to the photos of gas welds in this chapter. With just a little practice, you'll be able to create welds as good as any pictured here.

Acetylene gas pressure for welding thin-wall 4130 steel tubing should be set at 4 to 6 psi. *Richard Finch*

Oxygen pressure should be set at the same number at which acetylene pressure is set for *neutral-flame* gas welding, about 4 to 6 psi, *not* higher. *Richard Finch*

Welding is an acquired art. When you are learning to make good aircraft-quality welds, think about what you are doing. Think about the exact time to dip the rod into the puddle to make the fitted seam one continuous, smooth piece of metal. And you gas-weld each tubular joint one dip of the welding rod at a time.

COMMON GAS-WELDING MISTAKES

For beginning gas welders, the most common mistake is trying to melt off pieces of the welding rod and drop the melted pieces onto the seam, hoping the parts will glue themselves together. Even advanced welders still try to heat the welding rod. You will never learn how to weld if you persist at melting the welding rod.

The secret to good gas welds is to slightly preheat the weld area with the torch flame, then concentrate the flame where you want the first tack weld to be. Then, if your tip size is correct, within 3 to 5 seconds you should see a molten metal puddle forming on both pieces of metal to be welded. At that instant, dip the welding rod into the area where the puddle has formed, then pull the rod back out.

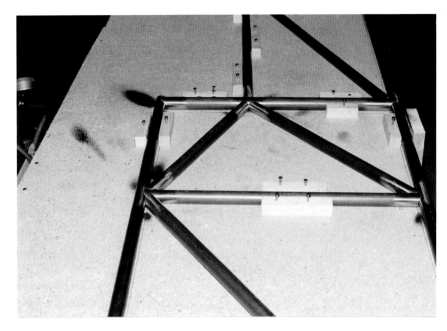

This 4130 steel-tube framework is laid out on a particleboard welding table for accuracy. Burn marks on the table are normal, and they indicate that another framework side has already been tack welded on this table. *Richard Finch*

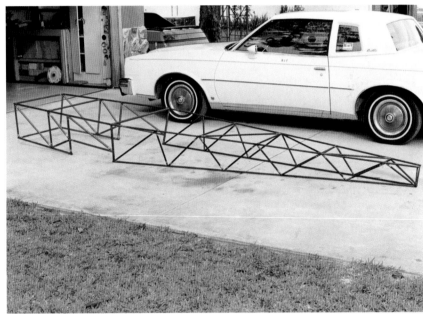

After two side frames are tack welded, they are assembled on yet another weld jig with cross members to form an airplane fuselage. After all the joints are tack welded, then final welding takes place, starting at the front and working aft. *Richard Finch*

You have just deposited one drop of weld rod into the weld. Then, each time you dip the rod into the puddle, a drop will melt off and flow into the weld, forming a weld bead. Maybe you can think of forming a weld bead as being similar to knitting a sweater. In knitting, each time you grab the knitting yarn, you make a stitch. Soon, with a consistent pattern, you will have a knitted sweater. And soon, if you keep a consistent pattern of forming and maintaining a puddle and dipping the welding rod into it, you will have a beautiful weld seam.

Another mistake that new welders make is burning holes in their weld. Good, tight-fitting fit-ups will do a lot toward preventing holes in the welds, but if one starts to melt in front of you, immediately pull the torch back 2 or 3 inches to reduce the heat on the weld. Then go back and quickly put weld rod material at the edge of the hole to cool it. Yes, welding rod cools the weld puddle. Usually you can fill small holes by welding over them, but if they get bigger, stop welding, cool the weld by waiting a couple of minutes, then make a small patch to cover the hole, and include the patch in your weld.

There is no fixed size to tell you when to make a patch over a hole, but use good judgment and don't weld a patch so small that it melts before you can

weld it into the structure. One rule of thumb is that a melted hole the diameter of a pencil needs a patch three times the diameter of the hole you are patching. Once you patch a hole, you'll try a lot harder to avoid burning holes in the future. And again, a tightly fitted tube is a lot less likely to melt into a hole.

BENDING TUBING

The most simple tubing benders are electricians' conduits, or "hickeys." You can buy three or four sizes of these manual conduit benders at your local builder's supply outlet. Most of these benders have a provision for screwing in a pipe handle. These benders work fairly well for putting mild bends (just a few degrees) into 1/2-, 5/8-, 3/4-, 7/8-, and 1-inch thin-wall 4130 steel tubing. They are designed to put 90-degree bends into EMT thin-wall electrical conduit. But they will collapse the wall of 4130 steel tubing if you try to put too tight a bend in it.

Several other types of tubing bending machines can do a good job of bending aircraft-quality tubing, but these hydraulic benders sell for $500 or more. If you're doing production bending, it might pay to invest in one of these benders.

Another bender that works well for small jobs is the three-roller adjustable bender. These can bend 1 1/4-inch diameter stainless-steel tubing into circles small enough to make a yacht tiller wheel, about 18 inches in diameter. That would be a 9-inch radius bend. Many shops make their own roller benders. The

This biplane was built by gas welding mild-steel tubing into an airplane structure. The left landing-gear leg attachment is shown here. *Richard Finch*

The firewall side of engine mount is a good example of how a sound gas weld should look when it's finished and painted. Note that the weld bead is three or four times wider than a TIG weld. *Richard Finch*

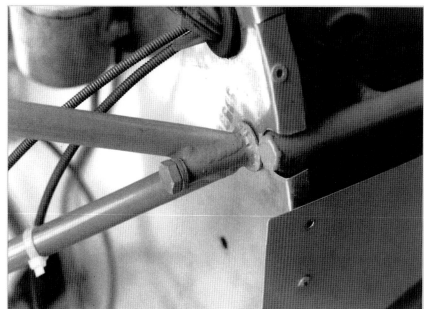

important thing is that each of the three rollers must be radiused to fit the tubing snugly to prevent the sides of the tube from spreading out and kinking. This means that each diameter of tubing you want to bend must have a special set of three roller dies to fit it. You can even bend 3-inch diameter 0.090-inch wall stainless-steel tubing to a 200-inch radius with one of these homemade tubing benders.

Another solution for one or two tubing bends, such as a race car roll bar or an airplane windshield bar, would be to take your tubing to a commercial tubing bending shop in your area. In any event, you ought to have a full-sized drawing of your desired bends. *Do not try to bend thin-wall tubing by heating it.*

RUST PROTECTION

For many years, welders were told to fill the inside of each welded tube in an airplane fuselage with linseed oil to prevent rust. Just imagine for a couple of minutes what would happen in a year or two when the tube developed a crack. The linseed oil would leak out all over the airplane fabric and ruin it.

And what if you decided to weld on a couple of small radio antenna brackets after the fuselage frame was completed and painted? All that linseed oil inside the tubes would likely catch fire, and it might even explode! So, do *not* fill your welded steel-tube structure with oil to prevent rust. It's a silly thing to do.

If the welds are solid, moisture will not get inside the tubes to cause rust. Any rust that might

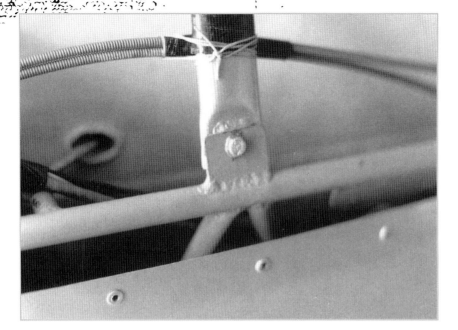

This gas-welded structural longeron fitting is the minimum quality you should try for. The welder who made this weld was very nervous! *Richard Finch*

One of the world's best aerobatic show biplanes is this 200-horsepower Pitts S1-A that was built by gas welding its 4130 steel fuselage and 4130 steel tail. *Richard Finch*

form will be from moisture on the outside of the tube, not inside.

Companies that weld tubular frames today explain that they believe the manufacturing oil that comes inside and outside new 4130 steel tubing is sufficient rust protection if you leave it inside the tubes and don't rinse it out with solvent. We've now debunked yet another old welder's tale about rust protection!

GAS WELDING STAINLESS STEEL

It is entirely possible to make pretty, strong, and sound welds on stainless steel with an oxyacetylene torch. To see what such welds look like, turn to this chapter's photo of the observation plane's exhaust pipe.

The secret to making sound gas welds like the ones pictured is to add a flange at the weld seam to keep the weld heat off the main part of the pipe. Because the flange sticks up, it's easy to heat it to its melting point without heating up the rounded part of the pipe. It is possible to add exactly the right sized flange so that the flange will be melted down to almost flat when the weld is completed.

A few companies that have been in business for many years furnish flux for gas welding stainless steel. These sources are listed in Appendix A.

BACKSIDE PROTECTION

As with TIG and MIG welding of stainless steel, it is important to protect the backside of your oxyacetylene

The rusted tubes in this trainer glider were restored by welding in new splices to replace the bad tubes, which were mostly in the bottom part of the fuselage. Interestingly, the rust was from the outside, there was no linseed oil inside any of the tubes. *Richard Finch*

Here is an excellent example of a gas-welded stainless-steel exhaust system on an observation airplane. Notice that the pipe was made from formed sheet, with two halves gas welded together. *Richard Finch*

welds on stainless steel. You can even use a small argon bottle and a flowmeter to argon purge the backside of your gas welds. It works the same with gas welding as it does with arc welding. If you don't have a suitable setup for argon purging, at least use one of the ceramic paste products listed in Appendix A to improve your stainless-steel gas welds.

STAINLESS-STEEL COLORS

Unlike chrome-moly steel, stainless steel does not produce the same color changes during the welding process. It does go from silver color at room temperature to black at 1,000°F, to dark red just before it begins to melt at 2,600°F. Stainless steel also starts to produce a black scale when heated to 1,600°F.

This black scaling is the primary reason for using flux when gas welding. Flux cleans off the scale, which prevents weld contaminations. This scale is like ashes, and it has no strength. Keep a small stainless-steel wire brush handy to clean the weld.

BRAZING STEEL

Always avoid brazing 4130 steel. The reason is because chrome-moly steel has a definite grain structure that actually opens up at medium-red brazing temperatures. When brazing alloy is melted onto the steel surface, it flows easily into the many small cracks and crevices in the chrome-moly steel. Then, as the braze joint cools, the brass will not compress, and it causes major cracks to form in the 4130 steel.

Often, a brazed 4130 steel part will crack completely in two before your eyes as it cools.

Mild steel (1020, 1025, etc.) is ready-made for brazing. It does not have the same kind of grain structure that 4130 steel does, so it won't crack when brazed at the correct temperature. The correct brazing temperature for mild steel is 1,250° to 1,350°F, which is a blood-red to cherry-red color. Any hotter and you will begin to boil the brass brazing rod (not filler rod).

Look at the photos in this chapter that show brazed race car frames. They are fitted exactly the same as a fusion-welded 4130 steel frame would be fitted, meaning no open joints and no wide gaps. By its nature, brass brazing rod loves to flow into seams measuring from 0.001 to 0.005 inch wide. Any wider and the capillary action of molten brass does not work. Keep your brazing joints as tight as possible.

Appendix A will give you suggestions for the best brazing rod for mild-steel thin-wall tubing. Be sure to note in the brazing rod specifications that the tensile strength of most brazing rod is 90,000 psi, which is stronger than the 60,000 psi of the mild steel that you braze with it. Brazing, when done correctly, can last as long as any other metal-joining method. And it can be as strong as fusion welding when done correctly.

To clean off the flux after the brazed joint is cool, use warm water to soften it, then wire brush it to remove the white flakes. A warm water-soaked rag works well for cleaning flux off a tubular frame structure.

Oxyacetylene brazing is being done here by a welder using flux-covered brazing rod. *Richard Finch*

This is Saturday morning of a weekend race car building project. The tubes were bent, notched to fit, and are ready to braze together. *Richard Finch*

This is Sunday afternoon on the weekend race car frame-brazing project, without any helpers. This point in the frame project represents about 20 hours of bending, fitting, and brazing.
Richard Finch

The race car frame in this photo is 99 percent brazed mild-steel tubing, including the suspension A-frames.
Richard Finch

The completed race car frame, minus the lightweight fiberglass body, required 12 months of part-time work to complete. *Richard Finch*

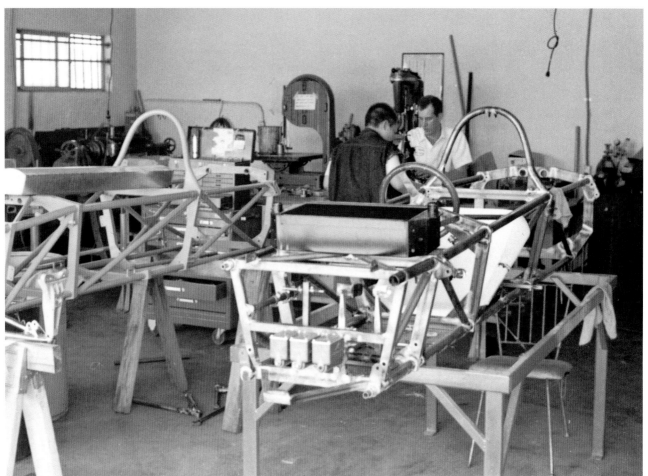

The LeGrand Formula Ford race car factory brazed these mild-steel-tubing Formula Ford frames because brazing is a stronger and faster fabrication method than fusion welding. *Richard Finch*

BRAZING NEGATIVES

Brazed joints can be weak if too little rod is used to make the joint. If you make sure to build up a good fillet of brass on the joint, weakness will not be a problem. Brazing is not strong enough to use for butt joints. Always make sure to provide for a fillet of brazing material to ensure a strong joint. The flux residue that adheres to the braze joint after the metal cools is a nuisance, and if you don't clean it off completely, it will continue to slowly flake off, even years later. If the part you brazed will fit in a water tank, soak it in warm water for 15 minutes after brazing and then the flaky flux will simply wire brush off.

STAINLESS-STEEL BRAZING

For many stainless-steel assemblies, brazing can be a completely adequate process, and the brazed joint will be stronger than the stainless-steel base metal. But not just any brazing rod will work on stainless steel. You need a high silver content brazing material to stick to stainless.

CHAPTER
10

GAS
WELDING
ALUMINUM

est-kept-secret is a very good way to describe the
mysterious (to many people) process of gas
welding aluminum. Most books that advertise to teach
you how to weld aluminum merely tell about the
obsolete alloy identification numbers such as 2S, 3S,
and other useless information. Next, they tell how to
weld thick pieces that have to be V-grooved with three
or four weld passes. They say nothing about how
to weld aluminum hoods on cars, aluminum nose
cowls on airplanes, or aluminum nose cones on older
race cars. So you'll learn about these previously untold
things in this chapter.

GAS WELDING LIMITS

Any aluminum welding projects that include metal
thicknesses over 1/4 inch or under 0.050 inch should
not be gas welded. Sure, it is possible to gas weld
thicker or thinner aluminum than these limits, but it's
better done with TIG welding. It is possible to tack
weld your parts together and then take them to a
commercial welding shop for finish TIG welding, but it
would actually be easier to simply jig the parts so the
TIG welder can weld everything without worrying
about heat distortion from tack welds. Each project
should be evaluated individually, but as an example,
if building a 5/16-inch 6061-T6 plate gearbox housing
for an auto-engine conversion, do not even try to gas
weld the project. But if welding a 1/8-inch 6061-T6
engine-mount bracket for a racing go kart, expect to
do that gas welding project with very little difficulty.
The only way you'll learn your own personal
aluminum-gas welding limits is to practice welding on
pieces of scrap aluminum.

EQUIPMENT REQUIRED

A standard oxyacetylene torch setup and a gas-
welding green-eye goggle will work OK for welding
aluminum. Names and contact information
for aluminum welding rod suppliers can be found
in Appendix A. You will also need a jar (not a can)
of aluminum-welding flux.

But the ideal setup for gas welding aluminum is an
oxy-hydrogen gas set and a cobalt blue lens for your
welding goggles. The reason that hydrogen gas works
better than acetylene gas is that hydrogen burns with
a mostly colorless flame. You'll be able to see the weld
puddle better, and you'll be able to better control the
fusion process.

A cobalt blue welding lens works best here
because it filters out the bright yellow light coming off

the weld so you can see the puddle better. Even if you
must use acetylene rather than hydrogen, the blue lens
will make your aluminum welds much easier to see,
and therefore easier to do.

HYDROGEN GAS

If you plan to gas weld aluminum on a regular basis,
you can set your shop up for oxy-hydrogen welding.
You will also need to keep an acetylene setup for
welding steel because hydrogen and steel welding
don't mix. Hydrogen in steel welds causes hydrogen
embrittlement and cracks.

You'll need to purchase a second high-pressure
gas regulator and gauges like the ones you already
use for your oxygen bottle. You shouldn't use your
oxyacetylene hoses because you need a hose setup
with both hoses for right-hand threads. Or you can
convert the second high-pressure regulator to acety-
lene-type left-hand hose fitting threads, but if you
do, put a permanent tag on the regulator that says
"Hydrogen Gas Only" so you don't try to hook it up
to your oxygen tank by mistake.

You'll also need to lease or buy a high-pressure
hydrogen tank filled with hydrogen gas. As a matter of
interest, a local city bus company has converted
several gasoline-engine-powered buses to operate on
compressed hydrogen gas rather than gasoline.
Hydrogen is very flammable, so treat compound
hydrogen as you would any potentially explosive gas,
with great care. One of the characteristics of hydrogen
is that it burns clean with no residue, but it could
explode "clean" if heavy concentrations of vapors
are ignited.

You don't need to make any changes to your
gas torch in order to burn oxy-hydrogen in equal
amounts for welding aluminum. Because aluminum
requires more heat to preheat for welding, you should
use one size larger tip than for welding the same
thickness steel.

OXY-HYDROGEN FLAME

You will need to adjust the oxy-hydrogen welding
flame exactly the same way you adjust an
oxyacetylene flame. Open the hydrogen valve on the
torch first (with 4 to 6 psi pressure) and light a flame
with a spark-type striker. Then open the oxygen valve
at 4 to 6 psi pressure, and adjust for a neutral flame.

The flame will be nearly colorless, but you'll be
able to see a very faint inner flame cone burning at
5,400°F, rather than 6,300°F as with acetylene.

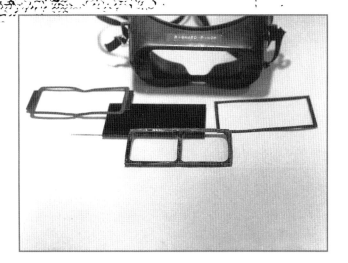

Special cobalt blue gas-welding lenses are much better for welding aluminum than the standard green tint lenses. Specify a number 3 tint lens. Also shown in this photo is a prescription-ground lens made for welding goggles. *Richard Finch*

This Smiths aircraft-sized torch works very well for welding aluminum. The torch barely weighs 9 ounces. *Richard Finch*

And once again, before you attempt to weld a real project with oxy-hydrogen, practice on several pieces of scrap aluminum until you get the feel of how the hydrogen flame reacts on the metal.

REAL PROJECTS

There is only one secret to making good welds in aluminum. The secret is that there is no telltale color change in aluminum as it's heated from room temperature to its welding temperature of 1,250°F. It only changes from dull to shiny just before a puddle forms. Learn this simple fact, and you'll be well on your way to becoming proficient at gas welding aluminum.

FLUX

Aluminum oxidizes (the equivalent of rusting) as it's heated. The only way to remove this oxide film is to completely bathe the weld seam with a flux that will inhibit and effectively prohibit oxides from forming. Flux-core aluminum welding and brazing rod is very effective. No extra flux is needed for most aluminum welding jobs when using this rod. The only negative thing about flux-filled aluminum brazing rod is that it has a bond strength of 28,000 psi, but it does have a tensile strength of 50,000 psi. One of the good points about using flux-cored aluminum brazing rod is that it has a very high melting point of 1,080° to

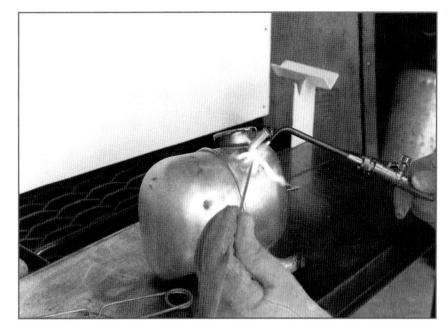

Using the Smiths torch and a small tip with a soft flame, this welder is repairing a loose tube in this Corvette radiator overflow tank made of 5052 aluminum. *Richard Finch*

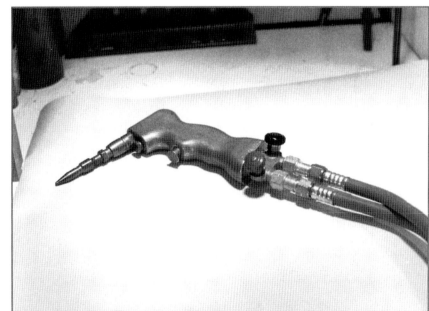

Another type of gas welding torch is this Dillon/Henrob unit that weighs 32 ounces, three-and-a-half times heavier than the Smiths torch, but it produces a more pencil-tip flame for delicate aluminum welding. It also has flashback arrestors at the torch adjustment valves.
Richard Finch

1,100°F, which means it will stand as much heat after welding as the base metal aluminum does at a temperature of 1,217°F.

Separate aluminum welding fluxes are also available. You usually mix these dry powder fluxes with water or denatured alcohol to form a liquid paste that can be brushed on the base metal and on the aluminum welding rod.

PARENT METAL RODS

When aluminum welding of car bodies, fenders, hoods, and trim was common back in the 1930s, the only way to find a positively compatible welding rod was to shear off a very narrow strip of the actual aluminum sheet that was to be welded. If the metal was S2, 18-gauge, then you had a piece of S2, 18-guage welding rod to use. And, of course, you needed lots of flux and a good stainless-steel-bristle wire brush to clean your welds. This method is still workable for welding aluminum. The problem with it is that you must first have a spare sheet of the correct weldable aluminum, and you must have a 4-foot-wide metal shear that will accurately shear off thin strips of that sheet aluminum. Tin snips can be used to cut thin strips if necessary. However, with modern metallurgy, this time-honored aluminum welding procedure is

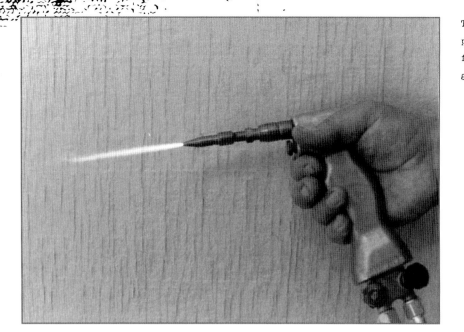

The Dillon/Henrob torch produces a pencil-tip flame rather than a feather-shaped flame common to most gas-welding torches. *Richard Finch*

no longer really necessary. You can just go to a welding supply house and buy a few sticks of appropriate aluminum welding rod.

NOW, THE PROCEDURE!

Here's the part you've been waiting for—how to gas weld aluminum and magnesium!

1. Brush the flux paste on the weld seam area, but only about 4 inches of length at a time.
2. For thin butt welds, clamp a copper backup strip to the back of the weld so you won't burn holes in the aluminum sheet.
3. For just five or six seconds, bathe the weld torch flame on the weld joint to slightly preheat the aluminum. Be sure you have flux paste on the seam.
4. Now you're ready to weld. Point the torch at the weld with a 45-degree angle to the seam, not 90 degrees as with steel welding.
5. The second that you see the aluminum get shiny and start to melt, immediately dip one or two drops of aluminum weld rod into that shiny puddle, then pull the rod back out and pull the torch back an inch or so to cool the weld.
6. Keep repeating step 5 until you have a good stitch weld in one area, then move to another area of the seam and start over at step 1 again.
7. With this process, you should be able to weld a 10-inch-long seam in 0.040-inch aluminum sheet in five to ten minutes.

Another trick of aluminum welding is to lay the torch flame nearly parallel to the surface of the seam if you tend to melt holes in the seam. You also may find that you can melt a couple of drops of weld rod off and onto the seam, then use the torch to flow the drops into the fusion of the seam.

TACK AND STITCH WELD

It is very important to tack weld several spots along the seam of any thin metal part to control warpage, and this is especially true with welding thin aluminum. And even after you tack weld several places along the seam, you should stitch weld short welds about 1/2-inch long, skipping 1/2 inch, then stitch weld again. Then, after you've stitch-welded the entire seam, hammer form the inevitable warped places back into shape, and then weld fill in the gaps between the stitches. Once you get the hang of it, gas welding aluminum will be just another kind of welding. But be sure to wash and wire brush all the flux off the weld seam to prevent future corrosion caused by the flux.

FLANGE WELDING

Where the design of the part will allow it, as in gas tanks, water tanks, and air-duct work, try to incorporate a 90-degree bent-up flange at the weld bead. The flange height should be about double the thickness of the sheet aluminum. If you are welding 0.040-inch aluminum, the flange should be about 0.080 inch high. The trick is to butt the two flanges together and just melt them together and down to almost the base metal level.

A dirty tip on the Dillon/Henrob torch causes a misshapen flame. Note the welding table torch holder that provides a safe place to hang a lighted torch while repositioning the parts to be welded. Never lay a lighted torch down. It could start a fire in your shop. *Richard Finch*

You will find that aluminum water tanks and fuel tanks are very easy to weld if you provide this meltdown flange for all the welded seams. The reason that it works so well is that the heat of the torch is only concentrated on the edge of the flange and away from the base metal. You will not tend to burn holes if you try to flange weld most thin aluminum assemblies.

ALUMINUM BRAZING

With the advent of new metallurgy and new aluminum alloy combinations, it is becoming easier and easier to produce good, high-strength braze connections in aluminum and magnesium. So try a few samples of aluminum braze materials and test the samples to destruction to see if this process will work for your projects. Appendix A gives examples of brazing rod and compatible materials along with material strengths.

OTHER USES

For a number of years, oven-furnace brazing of aluminum radiators, aluminum air conditioner evaporator cores, and other products has become very common because of the relative simplicity of applying brazing flux and metal powder to an assembly, heating the assembly to slightly above the brazing alloy melting point, but below the aluminum alloy melting point.

A notable use of aluminum brazing is the research-and-development practice of quickly cutting 0.100-inch-thick aluminum sheet into computer-drawn patterns that are then stacked and furnace-brazed into one solid piece, producing experimental auto engine blocks and cylinder heads. These experimental parts can be designed and fabricated in a matter of a few days compared to weeks or months for full, solid castings. Aluminum brazing opens up lots of possibilities for research and "ones" and "twos" projects.

PLASMA CUTTING

The traditional method of cutting steel with an oxy-acetylene torch is almost made obsolete by the new lightweight plasma torches that are available now.

For one thing, the oxy-acetylene cutting torch, commonly called the gas cutting torch, is basically a high-temperature flame that is augmented by a high-pressure stream of oxygen, which "oxidizes" steel. Since aluminum, brass, copper, and stainless steels will not oxidize or rust, these metals could not be cut with a gas cutting torch.

If you are cutting a piece of 2-inch thick steel with a cutting torch, however, you can start the cut with acetylene assisted by the high pressure stream of oxygen, and then you can actually shut off the acetylene flame completely and continue the cut with only the oxygen stream, while maintaining the cut and resultant heat in the metal. This is a demonstration of real oxidizing. If you were cutting a lot of 2-inch steel, you could save a lot of acetylene this way! Just for fun, try this "oxygen only" cutting method sometime. While cutting thick steel with oxygen and acetylene, simply reach over and turn the acetylene valve off. If you are smooth, the cut will continue even better with oxygen only than it was doing with acetylene.

Plasma cutting on the other hand, uses a very high temperature to locally melt the metal and employs a stream of high pressure gas to actually blow away the small, narrow kerf of melted metal, even more cleanly than the oxy-acetylene flame can cut. In fact, plasma cutting temperatures are in the 50,000 degree range compared to only 6,000 degrees for the oxygen-acetylene torch. The high pressure (usually about 60 psi) air or bottled gas is used to literally blow away the molten metal in the heated zone.

HOW DOES THE PLASMA TORCH WORK?

Inside that lightweight little metal box, is a miracle of electronics engineering. You simply plug the grounded 110 volt plug into a duplex receptacle, plug in to your air compressor, and then you have 50,000 volts of electricity that comes out of the gun, ready to melt any kind of metal and cut any shape you can think of. That's 110 volts in, and 50,000 volts out! If you simply must know how that is possible, you can call the manufacturer and ask to talk to a customer service engineer. We won't tell you about the physics in this chapter.

Plasma can melt any metal, starting with steel, then aluminum, copper, brass, stainless steel, cast iron, and even titanium. A regular cutting torch will only cut metals that will oxidize, such as steel.

The plasma torch initiates its own arc that is much hotter than any melting point of any metal. But even when cutting metals with high heat transfer, such as aluminum, the air blowing through the metal acts to cool the metal being cut so that you can usually hold the part being cut just seconds after you sever it. When you plasma cut very thick metal parts, they will be hot enough afterwards to need time to cool or a dip in a cooling bath.

WHAT CAN YOU CUT WITH PLASMA?

To test the set up on the torch used in this chapter, a piece of .010-inch thin aluminum sheet was cut. The cut came out perfect with very little dross, which is the metal that sags through on the back side of the cut. The dross can easily be sanded off with a small power sander. And the kerf, or cut slot was very narrow and neat, only about .050-inch wide. The really important thing about cutting the thin aluminum sheet was that there was no warpage of the cut. Even cutting with a set of tin snips left a wavy, warped line where the cut occurred. Another big advantage of cutting a similar sheet of .040-inch aluminum, was that the cut could be made with a straight edge made from a piece of 1x4-inch wood. The heat from the cut did not even scorch the wood. One NASCAR race shop fabricator regularly uses a piece of straight particle board as a guide for cutting sheet metal with their plasma torch.

The second thing that was cut with the torch was a piece of 1/4-inch thick steel plate. There was no change to the cut set-up other than to turn up the power to about double the setting that was used for cutting the aluminum. And again, there was a slag or dross that dropped through on the back side of the cut. The drop through is just a part of plasma cutting. Therefore, you need a small air operated angle sander to clean up the parts after you cut them with plasma.

COSTS OF A PLASMA CUTTING SET-UP

The plasma cutting equipment that was used in these demonstrations, the 110 volt *Lincoln Electric "Pro-Cut 25"* will cost you about $1,200 ready to take out of the box and plug in. You will also need an air compressor that will put out about 60 psi or more and be able to maintain the air flow for as long as you need to cut.

This student draws an elk head on his laptop computer while his dad looks on. Anthony uses *Corel Draw 9* to generate images that can be transferred to the Torres Welding Shop pantograph plasma cutting machine. *Richard Finch*

You can see a plasma cutting torch clamped to the pantograph cutting machine. The machine takes commands from the laptop computer and transfers x and y dimensions to the torch and to the electric servo motors, to move the plasma torch to make intricate cuts in a 1/2-inch steel plate as you see here. *Richard Finch*

The laptop computer is hooked up to the control cables to make the plasma torch start the cut, to move at a correct speed for the thickness of steel or any other metal, and to stop when the cut is completed. Plasma cutting produces lots of sparks, but very little heat in the metal. *Richard Finch*

Usually, any air compressor that will support a spray paint gun will also support a plasma cutter.

The compressor that was used in these demonstrations was a 1 horsepower, 2-cylinder unit that puts out 5.4 standard cubic feet of air per minute. Most welding shops will already have an air compressor of this capacity, but they cost about $450 retail.

PLASMA CUTTING HINTS

Hole piercing: Even the most expensive plasma cutters will blow back a small amount of metal just before the hole blows through. Often this is no problem, but if you must have a perfect cut, then drill a 1/8-inch hole in the metal where you want to start the cut. Then just start your cut at the edge of the 1/8-inch hole. There will not be any blow-back by doing it this way.

Laying out the cut lines: If you are used to having to use soapstone to draw cut lines on metal when using an oxy-acetylene cutting torch, then you will be very pleasantly surprised to know that a simple little Magic Marker pen or a Sharpie pen will work great for drawing the cut line on any metal when plasma cutting. The cooler cutting temperatures of plasma cutting make this possible.

Dry air is a necessity: If you allow water to get into the plasma cutter torch, it will drastically shorten the life of your consumables (the copper tips in the plasma cutting gun/torch). Make sure that you have a good quality water trap at the air inlet to the machine. We used a mechanical water trap, plus a disposable water trap in the air line.

This sheet of metal is 1/8-inch-thick mild steel and was 4x8-feet overall dimension before the plasma cuts were started. Here you see that the student had programmed the laptop computer to cut out several duplicate elk heads plus his favorite car symbol, the bowtie. *Richard Finch*

Fishmouth fitting tubing: If you have been using a tubing notcher to fit tubing for a tubular frame or engine mount, try marking your desired cut line on the tube with a Sharpie pen and then cutting just ahead of the cut line with a plasma cutter. After the plasma cut is made, clean up the cut with an air-operated die grinder and an angle sander. You may find that you can fit tubing a lot faster and more accurately with a plasma cutting torch. Try it, you may like it!

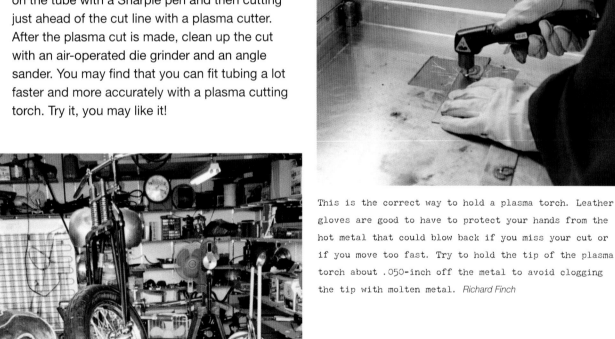

This is the correct way to hold a plasma torch. Leather gloves are good to have to protect your hands from the hot metal that could blow back if you miss your cut or if you move too fast. Try to hold the tip of the plasma torch about .050-inch off the metal to avoid clogging the tip with molten metal. *Richard Finch*

The man above is cutting a flame design from aluminum sheet. The aluminum flames will be dressed and polished to make a cover for a hidden gas tank filler cap for the chopper motorcycle on the stand behind John. *Richard Finch*

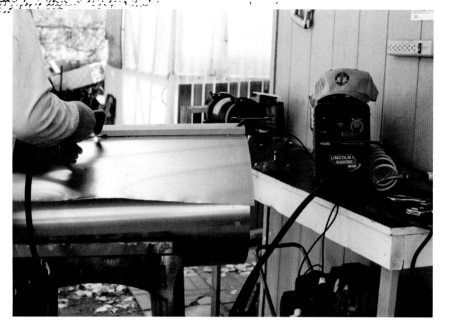

A large roll of .040-inch No. 5052 weldable aluminum is being cut in order to build a cold tank for cleaning automatic transmission cases. Notice 1x4-inch piece of wood used as a straight edge to guide my cut. Plasma cutting allows for the use of a wood guide because plasma is a much cooler cutting process. *Gayle Finch*

There are a lot of sparks coming from this cut in the 1/2-inch-thick steel air conditioner compressor bracket that is being cut here. Note that an 110-volt *Lincoln Electric "Pro-Cut 25"* plasma cutter was used used to cut the thin aluminum sheet with. It will also cut up to 2-inch-thick steel plate. *Gayle Finch*

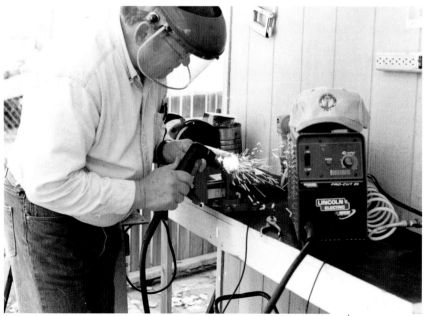

It is a lot easier to cut a saddle or fishmouth shape on a piece of steel tubing, using a plasma cutter, than it is to set up the same cut with a milling cutter or a hole saw cutter. Just draw the line shape you want to cut with a marker and cut on the line. *Gayle Finch*

Here is the piece of steel exhaust pipe tubing that was cut with the plasma cutter. Now, the rough edges of the cut can be cleaned up with an air die grinder or an air angle sander. The cut took less than 20 seconds to complete, much faster than the hole saw method, but not quite as smooth as the hole saw cut. *Richard Finch*

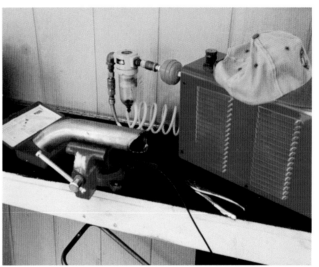

The only consumables that are used in plasma cutting are these copper electrodes (on the left), and the copper nozzles (in the center compartment). They only need to be replaced when they become clogged from molten metal blowing back into them. The cup in the right side compartment is just a spare. In welding terms, consumables are things that you use up, like welding rod. *Richard Finch*

Note that two water filters are installed in the air line that supplies 60 psi of regulated shop (air compressor) air to the plasma cutting machine. The first water trap can be drained when it gets partly filled with water, but the smaller filter is a disposable one that you throw away and replace. *Richard Finch*

CHAPTER
12

SHIELDED METAL
ARC welding

For about 70 years, the people who welded things using the arc and wire electrode method of welding, called their work "stick welding." The name was derived from the thick wire electrode, the "stick," that was used in the process. The proper name for the process is shielded metal arc welding (SMAW). The process is popular for simple backyard projects, such as BBQ grills and simple tables, where the strength of the weld is not crucial.

Stick welding rod is usually 1/8-inch diameter at the bare end, where you clamp it into the rod holder, also known as the stinger. The organic coating that covers the business part of the rod, which is also known as the flux, will be larger in diameter, usually about 3/8-inch in diameter. Before flux coated rod was invented, the best stick welding rod was actually rod that had a significant coat of rust on it. The rust formed a protective cover over the molten weld bead somewhat like the flux coating does these days.

STICK WELDING EQUIPMENT

Any TIG Welder that is used to weld steel can also be used to stick weld. You simply unplug or disconnect the TIG torch and connect a stick welding stinger and you are set. With a TIG machine, you will have the ability to use three different polarities: DC straight, reverse polarity (DC -), DC positive (DC +) and AC. AC reverses polarity 60 times per second using 60-cycle power. A machine set on 400-cycle power would reverse polarity 400 times a second. For the project in this chapter, a Square Wave TIG welding machine that operates off of 220 volts and 60-cycle power was used.

The only stick welding machines that are worth using are the 220-volt, 175-amp and above models. Don't waste your time on an inexpensive machine that is rated for 50 amps and below. There are some new high-end inverter powered welders that can be plugged into 110-volt, 20-amp circuits and then weld at 140 amps and above. Inverters are truly miracles of modern technology. The newer inverter 110–220-volt machines are usually no larger than a lunch pail and weigh about 25 to 35 pounds, compared to older 300-amp machines that can weigh 400 pounds or more.

STICK WELDING ROD

For the average shop, the only rod numbers you need are E6011 for dirty work and E7018 for clean work. The versatile E6011 will weld anything, including oily, rusty, painted steel. But it spatters almost as much as it welds. It is a good welding rod for beginners

because, when using it, the arc is easy to start and maintain. You can even weld over a previous weld without cleaning off the flux before you weld. But E6011 is mostly for mild steel such as angle iron that has less than 60,000 psi tensile strength. The number 6011 denotes that the rod has 60,000 psi tensile strength and is all-position, meaning you can weld flat, uphill, or upside down. It is the rod for beginners and for those quick and dirty jobs that you may want to throw away soon.

The more durable E7018 on the other hand, is the rod of choice for building the plumbing in nuclear power plants. The professional welders have a saying "TIG in, stick out," meaning that they weld the first pass of a high-pressure steam pipe with 90,000 psi tensile strength bare 4130 steel TIG rod, and then finish welding the pipe with multiple passes of stick welding rod, usually E7018. One of the main problems with E7018 rod is that it is easy to include pockets of slag in the weld. ALL the first-pass slag (or flux) MUST be completely removed before running the next weld bead in a multi-pass weld. But in most small shops, you usually only run one pass anyway, so slag is no problem. Even if you run multiple passes, your welds won't be subject to X-ray inspection (unless you work in a nuclear power plant). Just do a good job of chipping off the flux and then wire brush thoroughly before making the next pass/bead of weld.

The E7018 rod can be used by machines set in all positions on AC or DC reverse polarity. This rod can be hardened by heat-treating after welding. This rod is also called "low hydrogen rod" and should be kept dry at all times. Store it in moisture proof containers and preheat it to 200 degrees Fahrenheit for several hours before using it if it has become damp.

Welding rod sizes do make a difference in home shop welds. The 1/8-inch rod is the largest size that most shops should stock. The easier to use size is 3/32-inch rod (2.4 mm).

THINGS TO WELD WITH STICK

There will be many projects that will be best welded with stick welding rather than with TIG, gas, or MIG welding. For instance, the very useful "angle iron" is not easy to TIG weld because the metal contains lots of impurities. But angle iron welds nicely with E7018 stick electrodes. You can build shop equipment including tables, benches, carts, trailers, jigs and fixtures, and yes, even barbecue grills with stick welding. You can also use the more spatter-prone E6011 rod for the same projects.

This machine makes a great TIG welder,
and also is a solid stick welder. The
foot control and argon tank are not
used for stick welding. Most of the
welding was done at the setting you
see here, which is 80 amps. The 100-
amp setting is good for learning how
to start an the welding arc. Once you
have arcing down, turn the setting
down to 80 amps to weld.

Here the lathe table is finished and
painted. It was built so that a
factory-made roll around tool box
would just fit in, creating a neat
storage place for lathe and mill
tools. The shelves on the left side
are for holding sanders and grinders.

The legs and the framework on this lathe table were squared up using a carpenter's framing square. The table is turned on it's back for tack welding. Note the tacks on the under side of the top. Two-inch by two-inch angle iron was used for this project.

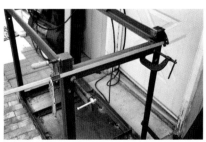

The table is being held square by several carpenter's clamps, machinist's clamps, and the framing square. The table is taking shape and most of the tacking and welding is being done with the table upside down.

Note in this picture that there is some flux and smoke around each tack weld. For prettier welds and stronger welds, chip off the flux and wire brush off the smoke residue before continuing the welds. The top was stitch welded because it was not necessary to have full welds to hold the top on.

WELDING SHOP
SAFETY

In the early days of welding and soldering, unfortunate workers melted and flowed lead all day long, every work day, and inhaled a lot of lead before they retired.

Now everyone knows better than to breathe lead fumes or otherwise expose ourselves to lead, but you still inhale small amounts of other toxic fumes from welding and metal-heating processes. Breathing welding fumes is a long-term danger, but other dangers are more near-term. Let's take a look at some of the immediate dangers.

BURNS

Welding generates very high heat, as much as 50,000°F for plasma cutting, and at least 2,700°F for simple fusion welding of steel. One of the most likely welding shop accidents would be to weld one part of a tubular structure and then immediately lean your arm on the extremely hot surface while bracing your arm to weld another tube nearby. The tube could still be as hot as 1,500°F down to 400°F. Leaning your bare arm on such a hot tube would cause a severe burn.

There are several solutions to the accidental burn problem. Wear long leather sleeves and leather gloves while welding tubular structures. Hang temporary tags that read Hot on each just-welded joint. And take more time to be sure which parts of the structure are still too hot to touch.

EXPLOSIONS

A very real and possible danger when welding race car and airplane parts is welding things that once contained flammable and explosive liquids. Never try to weld or apply heat or flame to any oil cooler, oil tank, fuel tank, or fuel line unless you know for sure that the item has been completely flushed and purged with an inert gas.

Washing out an oil cooler with cleaning solvent will not make it explosion-proof. Most oil and fuel tanks should be completely boiled out in a caustic type cleaning tank. Steam cleaning is not an effective way to make a fuel tank or oil cooler safe to weld on. Sometimes it's best to be smart and refuse to weld any tank, line, or radiator that has ever contained anything flammable. And believe it or not, 50/50 mixes of ethylene glycol antifreeze and water are highly flammable and explosive under the right conditions.

So, under what circumstances can you weld a used oil radiator or even a used air-conditioning evaporator that once had compressor oil in it? You must know for sure that it had been boiled out in caustic radiator cleaner. Then purge the tank or evaporator with an inert gas, such as argon, before and during the time you are welding it. Don't want to take a chance of a tank exploding in your face while welding it.

EYE FLASH

Another weld shop danger that can cause almost immediate pain is UV-ray eye flash from arc welding. Any electric arc produces ultraviolet rays, which are similar to those that cause sunburn. Eye flash is an insidious and serious problem. The first two or three times you get an eye flash from the welding arc, nothing happens. But after one to 12 hours, your eyes will begin to feel like somebody poured sand in them. The only way to ease the pain is a trip to a hospital emergency room or a physician to get some painkiller for your eyes.

After several welding eye burns, you will be in danger of eye cancer, or at least eye cataracts. You surely don't want that, so protect your eyes and your bystanders' eyes from this serious problem. One overlooked but serious problem with eye flash is your pets—cats, dogs, or any animal that may be fascinated by the bright light of the arc weld.

It is solely the welder's responsibility to shield his weld so that innocent beings, human and animal, are not accidentally exposed to the UV flash. Keep a small, foldable aluminum shield at your welding table to shield your arc welds. A secondary benefit of this portable shield is that it also shields your welds from potentially harmful air drafts.

WELDER'S CLOTHING

A good welder should have several different pairs of gloves. Keep one pair of dirty, greasy leather gloves to use when handling new tubing that has dirt and oil all over it. Also have a couple of pairs of cotton gloves handy for hand protection while operating tools and shop equipment, such as the band saw, the drill press, the hydraulic press, and the mill. One new, clean pair of canvas gloves is recommended for gas welding. So is a pair of very soft, very light gauntlet gloves specially made for Heliarc welding. Never touch a welding rod with dirty, greasy, oil-soaked gloves. And never weld with wet gloves. Oil, grease, dirt, and moisture on dirty or wet gloves will contaminate your welds.

WELDING HELMETS

Welding helmets come in as many styles and shapes and weights as dress shoes. The lightest helmets are

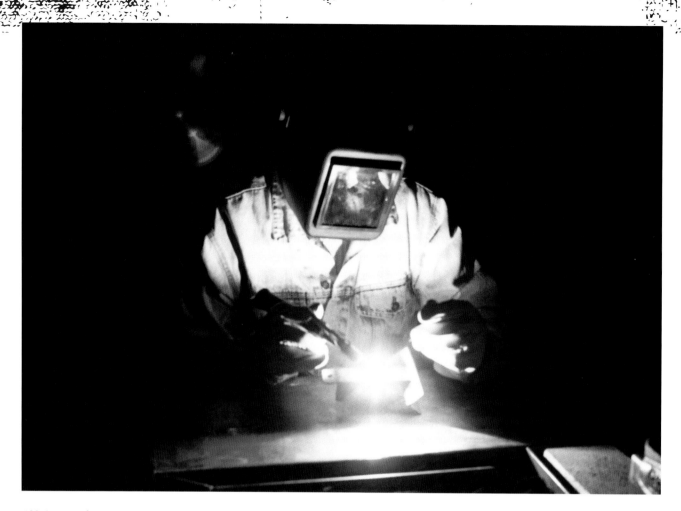

All kinds of arc welding, MIG, TIG, stick, and plasma are sources of ultraviolet radiation. This radiation will burn your skin and especially your eyes. So cover yourself completely, as shown here. *Gayle Finch*

so small that they don't fully protect your neck while welding. Get a larger, longer helmet with a big-window lens. Here are some things to look for in shopping for welding helmets.

- Lighter is better. A heavy helmet will tire you faster.
- A flimsy helmet and headband is bad.
- Buy a helmet for looks, too. This is important.
- Try an electronic lens helmet. You may want one. If you buy a bad, cheap helmet, you will never be happy with it. Invest a little more in a really nice helmet. Your welds will be better.

GAS-WELDING GOGGLES

Recent developments in gas-welding safety goggles have really improved the comfort and convenience of wearing eye protection while gas welding and brazing.

Two or three companies currently sell gas-welding goggles that look like a $200 pair of ski goggles, but are really high-quality welding goggles that sell for under $10. One manufacturer makes a gas-welding goggle that fits on your face like a nice pair of

sunglasses. And they fit your face tightly so sparks can't get inside. Check these new goggles out before you settle on the old-style models.

If you wear prescription eyeglasses, you must also wear a prescription goggle for welding. Ask your eye-care professional to show you special lenses for welders. If you can't read this page without prescription glasses, then you can't expect to weld without prescription lenses.

SHOP SAFETY

Clean your parts and your welding rod with acetone, which is almost as flammable as lighter fluid or possibly even gasoline. The procedure for doing this seemingly dangerous practice is to either clean your parts and your welding rod outside the weld area, or clean the parts, then remove the acetone from the weld area before you start welding. You will have to remind yourself often to keep all flammables out of the weld shop when you are welding.

Special breathing hoods are necessary when you are making lots of smoke and sparks with flux-core MIG welding. This welder is properly protected while SAW stick welding. *Sellstrom Manufacturing Company*

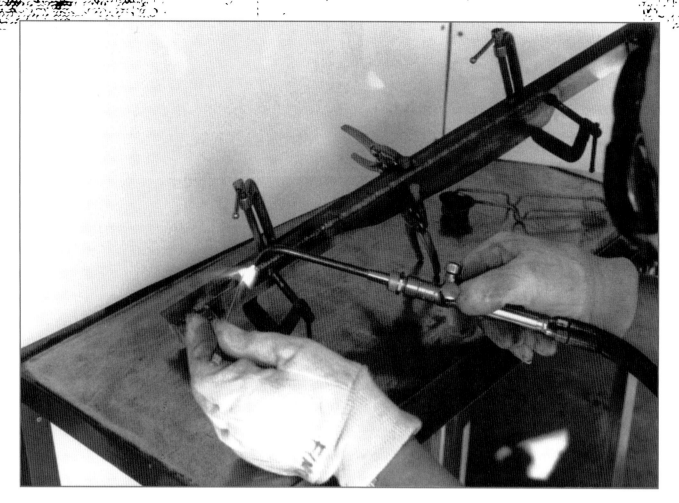

Cotton gloves work just fine for light-duty gas welding and brazing. For TIG welding, wear thin, flexible leather gloves for UV protection. Shield your welds against wind and arc exposure as was done here with a solid aluminum shield. *Richard Finch*

FIRE EXTINGUISHERS

Have one 2 1/2-pound dry-chemical fire extinguisher for your welding table, one on your gas-welding cart, one on the workbench wall, and one by the door to your shop. Also keep a garden-type water hose coiled and ready to use just outside. These precautions are cheap fire insurance, and if they are never needed, great. But they are also good peace of mind.

One negative thing about 2 1/2-pound dry-chemical ABC fire extinguishers: they really make a white powdery mess when you use them. So if your budget will allow, buy Halon 1301 or CO2 fire extinguishers for your shop and avoid the mess.

GENERAL SAFETY RULES

Never depend on sight or smell to determine if a container with unknown contents is safe to weld. If in the slightest doubt, clean the container thoroughly.

A rather shaky substitute for purging containers, tanks, coolers, and radiators for welding is to fill them with water to just below where the repair weld is to be made. It can be done this way, but purging is safer.

Never carry a full or empty acetylene bottle in the closed trunk of a car or inside a van or station wagon. Leaking acetylene fumes can explode with enough force to completely destroy a car, van, or station wagon. Always carry acetylene and flammable gas

This tub of clear water provides a tank to cool hot parts, and it also doubles as an emergency fire extinguisher.
Richard Finch

bottles in an open trailer, open truck, or open p ickup bed.

Hollow castings, containers, and closed tubes must be vented while welding on them to prevent them from exploding from heat expansion caused by welding.

Never weld, cut, or grind where the air may contain flammable dust, gas vapors, natural gas vapors, or flammable liquid vapors.

If there is *any* possibility of fire danger, such as making a weld repair directly on a vehicle or airplane, have a fire-watch person stand by while you are welding.

If you have a single doubt about fire or explosion safety on any weld project, *just don't do it*. Figure out

a way to remove the reason for the single doubt.

Drafts in weld areas are detrimental to the welds, but you should provide for a fume suction system when you are welding things that produce smoke and fumes. Sometimes a fan pointed outside in an open window will remove smoke and fumes sufficiently.

SKIN CANCER

Any exposed skin, especially the welder's throat area just below the neck, is susceptible to melanoma, or skin cancer, when repeatedly exposed to arc-welding UV rays. So, always cover everything on your body when MIG, TIG, or arc welding.

Welding rod comes in grades, just like nuts and bolts. That's right—you can buy cheap-quality welding rod or you can buy high-quality, certified welding rod. What's the difference?

Here's an example: Airplane builders typically spend $100,000 to build a fast, high-tech airplane. Then they spend $75,000 to purchase a new aircraft engine and propeller for the plane. Does it make economic sense to spend less than $5.00 for the welding rod that holds the plane's engine mount together?

You can go to your local welding supply store and buy one pound of no-name copper-coated steel welding rod for as little as $1.50. The welding supply store has no idea what the rod is made of, except that a magnet will stick to it, so it must be steel, not solid copper, aluminum, or stainless steel. It is also a fact that the cheap copper-coated steel welding rod is usually made from scrap metal—old cars, old bicycle frames, old tractor parts, and old concrete reinforcing bars salvaged for scrap. Not the kind of metal you'd want to hold an airplane engine mount together, or to hold the front suspension together on a 250-mile-per-hour Indy race car.

Find a manufacturer that sells nothing but high-quality, metallurgically controlled, vacuum-melted, rolled welding rod, and which furnishes certification papers with each lot of welding rod they sell. Yes, their price for 5 pounds of TIG welding rod will be 30 times more expensive than for 5 pounds of the cheap stuff. This means that one would have to spend $40 for one pound of 4130 steel welding rod to weld the engine mount that holds the $75,000 engine in the $100,000 airplane!

But even if you want to weld an engine mount to hold a $2,000 engine in a $10,000 airplane, $40 for the welding rod versus $1.50 for the cheap rod is not a high price to pay. Your own safety and well-being is surely worth the few extra dollars for the good welding rod.

RESULTS WITH CHEAP ROD

If cheap, reclaimed scrap welding rod is used to TIG or MIG weld 4130 steel, you can expect a number of defects in your welds. Cheap welding rod will bubble and boil and leave big holes of porosity in your welds because the cheap stuff has unknown foreign matter in it, including large amounts of dirt, slag, grease, and moisture.

The copper coating on cheap rod does not mix with steel, and it enters the weld puddle to cause defects such as crater cracking and hydrogen embrittlement from exposure to moisture trapped between the flaking copper and the cracks and crevices in the cheap rod.

COPPER-COATED ROD

In many places in this book, you've been advised to use copper as a tungsten arc-starting block, and to use copper strips as backup strips when welding thin sheets of steel, aluminum, and stainless steel.

Copper is used because it will not mix or fuse with steel or other metals. When used for a heat-sink backup strip, you don't have to worry about the copper sticking to the welded seam. When you use copper as an arc-starting block, you don't have to worry about the nice, sharp, pointed tip of your tungsten electrode trying to stick to the copper.

If you cut a cross-section out of a common piece of copper-coated-steel welding rod and magnify it 3,000 times, you will be able to see that the copper coating is not adhering to the rod, but flaking off. The copper coating is not a part of the rod.

Then why do manufacturers use copper to coat steel welding rod? Copper-coated steel rod will rust, so the copper isn't used as a rust preventative. Manufacturers coat steel welding rod with copper to help make the wire drawing/sizing dies last longer. Copper is used to lubricate the drawing dies. Manufacturers also use soaps and oils that become embedded in the wire as it is drawn through the dies to size it.

MC-GRADE WIRE

Metallurgically controlled welding rod and wire are made from new material with traceable and certified elements. The rod and wire are melted in vacuum-chamber furnaces to prevent atmospheric contamination, then they're drawn and sized through rollers that squeeze them down to the various designated sizes. During each drawing through rollers, the rod and wire are mechanically wiped clean with

143

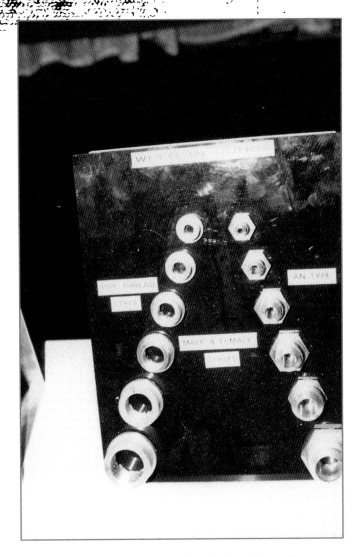

Weld-on fittings like the assortment shown here make an easy job of finishing aluminum oil tanks, fuel tanks, and water-recovery tanks. Buy an assortment of these fittings to have on hand for special welding projects. *Richard Finch*

MC-grade welding wire. This desiccant packaged 6 1/4-pound bag of vacuum-melt, metallurgically controlled welding wire is by far the best kind of welding rod to use on TIG welds for aircraft and race car projects. *Richard Finch*

acetone or denatured alcohol. No oils, soaps, or greases are used to lubricate the rollers. Only water is used to lubricate the sizing rollers.

At the final sizing for each batch, white-glove inspections are performed, and additional cleaning takes place before the rod is vacuum-packaged for shipment to customers. Now you can see where the extra costs comes from. And the real proof of quality comes in the welding. MC-grade welding rod makes a very good welder out of a relatively inexperienced welder. Cheap rod is hard to handle for even well-trained welders. If you still have cracks and porosity in your TIG and MIG welds, try some of the good stuff and see how fast you can become a great welder!

NUTS AND BOLTS

At the beginning of this chapter, the grades of welding rod were related to the various grades of nuts and bolts. You're probably aware of the no-markings bolts that you can buy at the hardware store. These bolts are made from steel of unknown origin, and they can twist and break very easily, so you don't want to use them for anything but lawn furniture. The next-higher-quality bolt grade is commonly used to hold bumpers and fenders on cars, SAE grade 5. Moving up in quality are bolts commonly used to attach cylinder heads to car engines. They have six marks on their heads, and they're SAE grade 8. Approximately equal in strength to SAE grade-8 bolts are AN bolts, specified for use in missiles and certified aircraft.

It's obvious that low-grade hardware-store bolts are cheaper than grade-8 and AN bolts, but quality nuts and bolts are more than worth the extra cost in safety-critical systems, such as aircraft and race cars. As with welding rod, never use the cheap stuff. Someone's life may depend on it.

EXPENSIVE COMMERCIAL GRADE

A number of welding-supply firms offer excellent welding rod and supplies. But be aware that, although a firm's name is on the packaging, that firm may not have manufactured the materials in question. Many firms contract with manufacturers to make welding rod and supplies and package them under their proprietary names. Except for the MSD sheets required by OSHA, these firms don't tell customers the exact metal and material content in their products. This practice is common in the welding supply industry. If you ask for certification sheets and can't get them, it is because another manufacturer makes the supplies and the second company repackages the product.

However, the fact that you pay $200 for 5 pounds of welding road does not guarantee a better product. For instance, one particular repackaging company sells a little wire tip cleaner for gas torches for $45; a local welding supply store sells the same wire tip cleaner for $4.50! It pays to shop for price and quality.

RECOMMENDED SUPPLIES

The remainder of this chapter is divided into sections of recommended welding supplies for TIG welding, then for MIG welding, then for gas welding. Finally, there's a section on general welding supplies.

WELDING GASES

At this time, there are several different methods of obtaining compressed gases for welding, acetylene, oxygen, hydrogen, argon, helium, CO_2, and combination mixed gases. Suppliers in different geographic regions vary in how they sell consumable gases.

One welding-gas retail dealer may lease only. This means that you pay a $125 deposit on each gas bottle, and a $10 monthly lease fee as long as you keep the bottle. You also pay $25 for the argon gas in the bottle. In one year, this dealer will get $270 from you for each bottle of gas you lease from him.

Just across town, another welding-gas retailer may sell you the same size bottle for $125, give you the first fill of argon free, with no monthly rent on the bottle, because you bought it. You can keep the bottle for a year and sell it to a friend or back to the dealer. So you saved $145 the first year on each bottle you bought rather than leased. As has been said before, shop around before you buy!

BOTTLE SIZES

Don't make the mistake of buying or leasing the very largest or the very smallest gas bottles, even if you're operating a full-time welding fabrication shop. The largest bottles will be a nuisance to handle, and the smallest ones go empty far too quickly. The following charts will help you decide the right size cylinders for your shop.

Bare TIG Rod for 4130 and 4140 Steel

*	USW Stock #6457V	Turbaloy 4130	for 4130 Steel
*	USW Stock #6452V	Turbaloy 4140	for 4130 Steel
**	LAC Stock #6457	AMS 6457	for 4130 Steel
***	A.S. Stock #4130T	æ	for 4130 Steel

Bare TIG Rod for Aluminum and Magnesium

*	USW Stock #4190C	5.2 Si	for 6061 and 5052 Aluminum
*	USW Stock #4181C	7 Si	for 356 Castings
*	USW Stock #1374C	5 Mg	for 5052 Aluminum
**	LAC Stock #4190	4043	for 6061 and 5052 Aluminum
**	LAC Stock #4246	AMS357	for 357 Castings
***	A.S. Stock #4043	æ	for 6061 and 5052 Aluminum

Bare TIG Rod for Stainless Steel

*	USW Stock #	AWS A5.9	for 308 Stainless
*	USW Stock #	AWS A5.9	for 316 Stainless
**	LAC Stock #S109	AWS A5.9	for 308 Stainless
**	LAC Stock #5692	AWS A5.9	for 316 Stainless

Bare TIG Rod for Stainless Steel

*	USW Stock #4914C	Alloy 15-3-3-3	Titanium
*	USW Stock #4951C	Alloy C.P.	Titanium
*	USW Stock #4952C	Alloy 6-2-4-2	Titanium
*	USW Stock #4954C	Alloy 6-4	Titanium
*	USW Stock #4955C	Alloy 8-1-1	Titanium
*	USW Stock #4956C	Alloy 6-4 ELI	Titanium
*	LAC Stock #4951	Alloy CP-Ti	Titanium
**	LAC Stock #4954	Alloy 6-4	AWS A5-16
**	LAC Stock #4956	Alloy 6-4ELI	AWS A5-16(4)

Bare TIG Rod for Magnesium

*	USW Stock #4350C	Alloy AZ61A	Magnesium
*	USW Stock #4395C	Alloy AZ92A	Magnesium
*	USW Stock #4396C	Alloy EZ33A	Magnesium
*	USW Stock #1308C	Alloy AZ101A	Magnesium
*	USW Stock #4350	Alloy AZ61A	Magnesium
*	USW Stock #4395	Alloy AZ92A	Magnesium
*	USW Stock #4396	Alloy AZ33A	Magnesium
**	USW Stock #M107	Alloy AZ101A	Magnesium

* United States Welding Corporation, Nevada
** Lancaster Alloys Company, California
*** ESAB All-State Welding Products, Maryland

Note: As the advantages of MC grade, vacuum-melt welding rod become better understood by welders, more new and old manufacturers will offer this superb welding material for sale. Meanwhile, do not settle for cheap welding rod for your expensive projects.

Tungsten Electrodes for TIG Welding

Name	Safety Concern	Use For
Pure Tungsten	Nonradioactive	Aluminum
2% Thoriated	Radioactive*	Steel, Stainless Steel
2% Ceriated	Nonradioactive	Orbital Welds
2% Lanthanated	Nonradioactive	Production
Tri-Mix Tungsten	Nonradioactive**	Steel, Stainless Steel

* Thoriated tungsten is radioactive. Extended exposure to radiation can cause cancer.
** Rare-earth mixtures do not contain radiation, yet offer better starting, less degradation, are cooler running, and misfire less on starting.

Note: Two percent Lanthanated tungsten is a rare-earth tungsten, is not radioactive, and offers benefits of improved arc starting, increased electrode life, and higher amperage-carrying capacity.

Two percent Ceriated tungsten is another nonradioactive rare-earth tungsten that is well-suited to autmatic orbital pipe and tubing welding.

Suggested Wire for MIG Welding 4130 and 4140 Steel

*	LEC Stock #L-50	AWS A5.18	for 4130 Steel
*	LEC Stock #L-50B	AWS A5.18	for 4140 Steel
*	USW Stock #6457V	AWS A5.18	for 4130 Steel
*	USW Stock #6452V	AWS A5.18	for 4140 Steel
*	LAC Stock #6457	AWS A5.18	for 4130 Steel

Suggested Wire for MIG Welding Stainless Steel

*	USW Stock #	AWS A5.9	for 308 Stainless
*	USW Stock #	AWS A5.9	for 316 Stainless
*	LAC Stock #3109	AWS A5.9	for 308 Stainless
*	LAC Stock #5692	AWS A5.9	for 316 Stainless

* United States Welding Corporation, Nevada
** Lancaster Alloys Company, California

TIPS FOR TIG WELDING

Check out the information in the gas welding section of this chapter that refers to fluxes. One company that supplies gas welding flux also recommends applying a thick paste mixture of its flux powder and alcohol to the backside of TIG welds on aluminum and stainless steel for vastly improved welds. Check out the Solar Flux data.

MIG Wire Continues to Change

MIG wire uses the same chemical mix of alloys as is used in TIG welding the same application. One current problem with MIG wire selection is that every significant company in the business is continuing to experiment with metallurgy to improve weldability of MIG wires. It would be wise to talk to a factory representative about your specific MIG welding requirements before investing in significant amounts of MIG welding wire.

Suggested Welding Rod for Oxyacetylene Steel

*	Oxyweld Stock #32-CMS	for 4130 Steel
*	USW Stock #6457V	for 4140 Steel
**	A-S Stock #RG-60	for 4130 Steel

* United States Welding Corporation, Nevada

** All-State, ESAB, Maryland

Do or Don't: Flux and 4130 Steel?

Gas welding(OFW), oxygen-acetylene welding of 4130 steel, does bit require any flux, and in fact attempting to use flux on the top side of the weld will make welding very difficult. However, it will aid the welding if a Solar Flux paste is applied to the back side of the weld to aid in heat control on thin sheet-metal butt welds. One difficulty in using flux on 4130 is the requirement that it be removed completely before welding the back side. For the average 4130 tubular structure, no flux should be used.

Flux-Core Aluminum Brazing Rod

Flux-core aluminum brazing rod is relatively new to the gas-welding field. When you use it to braze an oil tank made of 5052 aluminum, it is so close to the base metal tensile strength of 36,000 to 41,000 psi that it will give you welds as strong as fusion-welded aluminum. Actually the lowest tensile strength of 5052-O (soft) aluminum is only 29,000 psi. All of the flux-cored aluminum brazing rod listed in the previous table is above 30,000-psi tensile strength. The melting point of these flux-cored brazing rod is 1,050° to 1,100°F, just over 100°F lower than the 1,217°F melting point of the base metal, a difference that is not really controllable with a hand-operated oxyacetylene torch. Generally, you will end up with a good fused weld/braze joint anyway.

As in gas welding stainless steel, try to make each seam a 90-degree folded joint so that most of the heat is applied to the fold and not the flat base metal.

Suggested Welding Rod for Gas Welding Aluminum

1.	CWS Stock #CW1016**	35,000 psi	for 6061 Aluminum
1.	CWS Stock #CW1857**	34,500 psi	for 5052 Aluminum
2.	Welco Stock #COR-AL**	30,000 psi	for 5052 Aluminum
3.	USW Stock #1374C	5 Mg	for 5052 Aluminum

1. CRW is Cronatron Welding Systems, North Carolina
2. Welco is Thermacote - Welco Corporation, Michigan
3. USW is United States Welding Corporation, Nevada

** These aluminum rods are brazing rods, but the 30,000 to 35,000 psi tensile strength should be adequate for most fusion welding aluminum.

General-Purpose Solder

Cronatron No. 53 is a very low-temperature solder that melts at only 360 degrees F. And it will join all metals, aluminum to steel, copper, brass, stainless steel, etc., with a 17,500 psi tensile strength. This would be handy in unusual metal-joining situations. It requires a honey-consistency flux to work.

Suggested Welding Rod for Gas Welding Stainless Steel

USW Stock #CW1023	#95 Bare 95,000	TIG or Gas	

Suggested Welding Rods for Gas Brazing Mild Steel and Stainless Steel

CWS Stock #CW1002 #23F	Blue Coating	66,000	1,400–1,600°F
CWS Stock #CW1836 #30F	Pink Coating	100,000	1,300–1,600°F
CWS Stock #CW1025 #40F	Org (High Silver)	85,000	1,100°F
CWS Stock #CW1024 #43F	Blue Coating	88,000	1,100°F
CWS Stock #CW1017 #53	No Coat (All)	17,500	360°F

CWS is Cronatron Welding Systems, North Carolina

Note: 23F and 30F are for most regular steel and light cast iron brazing (economical). 40F is a high-priced but excellent high-silver-content silver brazing material that is excellent for stainless steel.
43F is a good, lower-cost silver conetnt brazing rod for steel, copper, brass, and stainless steel.

High-Pressure Cylinder
Oxygen, Argon, Helium, etc.

Cubic Ft.	OD	Height	Weight	Service Pressure
20	5.27"	14"	10 lb	2015 psi
40	7.0"	12"	23 lb	2015 psi
55	7.0"	23"	30 lb	2015 psi
80	7.0"	33"	42 lb	2015 psi
110	7.0"	43"	55 lb	2015 psi
125	7.0"	43"	55 lb	2065 psi
150	7.0"	46"	59 lb	2015 psi
220	9.0"	51"	114 lb	2015 psi
250	9.0"	51"	115 lb	2065 psi
300	9.27"	55"	135 lb	2400 psi
400	10.50"	66"	190 lb	2400 psi

Low-Pressure Cylinder Sizes for Acetylene

Number	Cubic Ft.	OD	Height	Weight	Service Pressure
S-10	10	4.0"	13"	7.5 lb	250 psi
S-40	40	6.0"	19"	23.4 lb	250 psi
S-75	75	7.0"	26"	43.8 lb	250 psi
S-145	145	8.0"	34"	74.1 lb	250 psi
W210	210	10.0"	32"	100.7 lb	250 psi

Recommended Gases for Welding

Welding Process	Suggested Gases
TIG Aluminum	Argon
TIG 4130 Steel	Argon
TIG Stainless Steel	Argon
TIG Titanium	Argon
MIG Aluminum	Argon
MIG 4130 Steel	75%-25% Argon and Helium
MIG Stainless Steel	Argon + 1% Oxygen
OFW Aluminum	Oxygen, Acetylene or Hydrogen
OFW 4130 Steel	Oxygen, Acetylene
OFW Stainless Steel	Oxygen, Acetylene
Inert Gas Purging	Argon

Be sure to ask your welding gas supply dealer to explain his special gas mixture to aid your MIG welding needs. Certain companies offer "Gold Mix," which is 70 percent argon, 12 percent helium, and 18 percent special mix, or other unusual percentage. Their experience tells them that even as little as 1 percent oxygen can greatly improve certain welding processes

Be sure to ask your welding-gas supply dealer to describe any special gas mixtures to aid your MIG welding needs. Certain companies offer gold mix, which is 70 percent argon, 12 percent helium, and 18 percent special mix, or other unusual percentages. The dealer's experience tells them that even as little as 1 percent oxygen can greatly improve certain welding processes.

Mil-Spec Fluxes

Below are listed a few of the better or best fluxes with descriptions of how each one works.

Solar Flux (1lb. Containers)	Type 1	For nickel, Inconel, etc. Mix with methanol to 1 pound form a thick paste. Works well to clean and to Containers protect the back side of gas, TIG, and MIG welds.
Solar Flux (1lb. Containers)	Type B	For all stainless steel. Mis with methanol to form 1 pound a thick paste. Apply to back side of gas, MIG, Container and TIG welds to assure sugar-free welds.
Solar Flux (1lb. Containers)	Type 202	For all gas welds on aluminum. Works well with TIG or MIG also. Makes gas welding aluminum easy.

Superior Flux & Manufacturing Company
6615 Parkland Boulevard
Solon, OH 44139
(440) 349-3000

No. 65
Flux for welding and soldering all metals except aluminum and magnesium. For air conditioners, refrigeration, stainless. 200–600°F.

Solar Flux (formerly Solar Aircraft, San Diego, California)
Golden Empire Corporation
144 Wayne Drive
Morehead City, NC 28557
(252) 808-3511

Bradford Derustit Corporation
17 Archer Drive
Clifton Park, NY 12065
(518) 899-5315

Derustit SS-3
Stainless-steel cleaner. Cleans heat scale off stainless-steel welds.

Bradford No. 1
Metal cleaner. Cleans steel, copper, brass. Rust oxide remover.

Backup Pastes for
Weld Protection and Jigging

HTP Stock #12084 Heat Sponge, Ceramic Heat Sink
CWS Stock #CW1082A Plio Jig, Ceramic Heat Sink
Check with your local welding supply retailer for 1- and 5-pound plastic cans of a moist, clay-like ceramic paste that will insulate your welds. These products work like putting a water-soaked rag by the weld to insulate the heat from the parts you don't want to overheat.

INDEX